PREHISTORIC ENGLAND

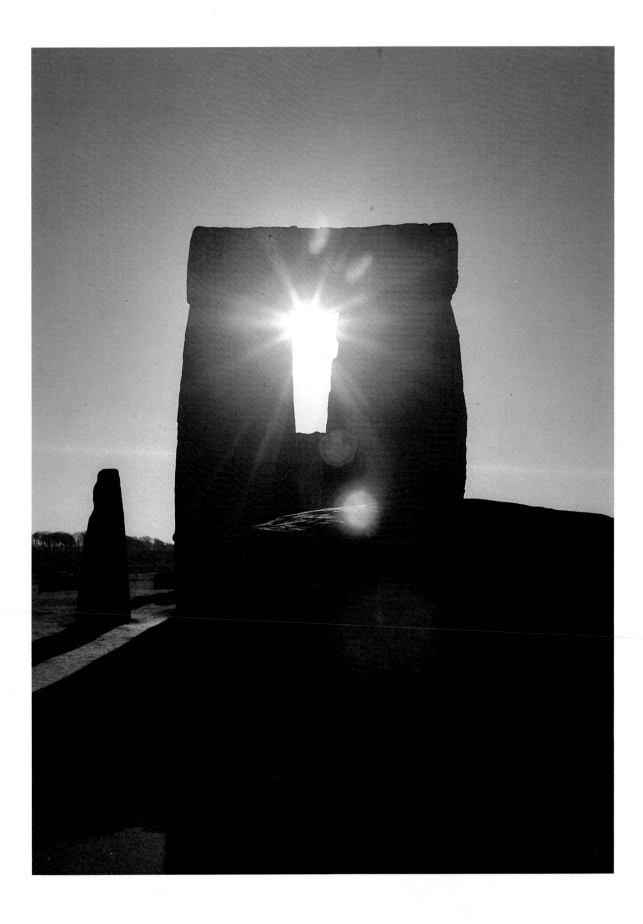

PREHISTORIC ENGLAND

RICHARD CAVENDISH

ARTUS BOOKS
LONDON

NOTE TO READERS

Many of the most interesting prehistoric sites in England are in the hands of the Department of the Environment or the National Trust, as indicated in this book, and are open to the public at reasonable hours. Other sites are on private land and the public has no right of access to them. Where there is no footpath or right of way, permission should be obtained to visit these sites.

It is up to us all to preserve England's heritage for future generations. Please follow the Country Code: do not cause damage of any kind to the sites or to crops, livestock, hedges, fences or anything else in the countryside; keep dogs on a lead whenever necessary; and please do not leave litter.

A coin of the Iceni tribe who occupied
East Anglia under Queen Boadicea
before the Romans came.

Copyright © Richard Cavendish 1983

Reprinted 1993

Artus Books, Orion Publishing Group, Orion House,
5 Upper St Martin's Lane, London, WC2H 9EA

ISBN 1 85605 169 2
Printed in Italy

CONTENTS

The Longstone on Dartmoor, an unusually slender monolith about 10 ft (3 m) high. It may be a fertility symbol.

INTRODUCTION:ENGLAND BEFORE THE ROMANS

TODAY'S England is the creation of generations of men and women over thousands of years, reaching far back into the drifting mists that conceal the remote past, long before the Romans came. We do not know the names or the life histories of the people of prehistoric England, but they have left us a landscape haunted by grey stone circles and mysterious standing stones, barrows and earthworks worn by time. This book is a guide to the most interesting, impressive and accessible of these sites. Places which are only of academic interest or which are unduly difficult to reach have been omitted.

Prehistoric sites are not spread evenly over the country. They tend to cluster on uplands and in areas away from the beaten track. This is not because prehistoric men and women lived only or mainly on high ground. The popular picture of them clinging timidly to the hilltops, too frightened to venture into the tangled forests below, is a travesty of the truth. Aerial photography has revealed traces of numerous prehistoric settlements in lowland England, destroyed by centuries of farming, building and industry. The sites that are left cluster on high ground simply because that is where subsequent occupation has least disturbed them.

Neanderthals and modern man

The human race evolved millions of years ago in Africa and spread into Asia and Europe. The first manlike beings in England arrived at least 300,000 years ago. They probably belonged to the adventurous, tool-making, fire-using stock known as *homo erectus* and they came across the land bridge that joined Britain to the rest of Europe in the Ice Age. At times the north of England, Scotland and Wales were covered by ice a mile thick. Mammoth and woolly rhino snorted and stamped in the Thames valley and herds of bison and reindeer foraged on the southern plains. However, there were long periods, called interglacials, when the climate was much milder. The oldest human bones in Britain date from one of these interludes. They are three pieces of the skull of a young woman, discovered at Swanscombe in Kent. She lived about 250,000 years ago and her kinsfolk hunted elephant and hippo twenty miles from where today's traffic thunders round Piccadilly Circus.

For thousands of years small groups of hunters roamed Britain as far north as the ice would permit, equipped with weapons of stone and wood. The oldest wooden implement in the world was found in England, at Clacton on Sea. It is a spearhead made of yew wood, of the same period as the Swanscombe skull. From about 70,000 BC a number of Neanderthal families occupied caves in England. Beetle-browed and heavy-jawed, expert hunters, with a brain capacity larger than that of some modern men,

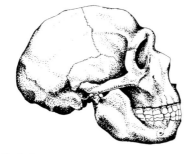 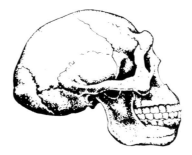 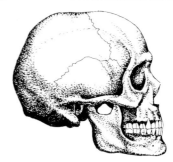

Left Reconstruction of a homo erectus *skull. These distant ancestors of modern humans were probably the first manlike creatures in England. They had broad, flat noses and receding chins, walked upright, made stone tools and used fire. Centre and right* Skulls of homo neanderthalensis *and* homo sapiens sapiens *or modern man.*

Artist's reconstruction showing a Neanderthal family round the fire in a cave they are using as a temporary home.

they made clothes from animal skins, buried their dead with ceremony and probably possessed coherent speech and a religion. They died out in England about 35,000 years ago, overtaken by – perhaps wiped out by – modern man, *homo sapiens sapiens*, our own direct ancestor.

Stone Age handaxes, so called, were all-purpose tools, with a magical mystique about them. This one, in the Devizes Museum, was a ritual object rather than a practical implement.

Barbed and tanged arrowheads, fastened to wooden shafts, were still in use in the early Bronze Age.

In about 12,000 BC the ice finally retreated and forests gradually clothed the land. The sea level rose until England was cut off from the Continent, somewhere around 7500 BC. The total population at this time was perhaps 10,000 people, with each small hunting band ranging over a territory of about 200 square miles (772 square km) of forest, paddling along the streams and rivers in dugout canoes. They lived on red deer and wild ox, wild boar, fox, hare and beaver, and by snaring birds and spearing fish.

Modern man developed more efficient and varied tools and weapons than his predecessors. These barbed fish-spears, found at Star Carr in North Yorkshire, are about 10,000 years old.

From hunting to farming

By about 4500 BC people had arrived in England who knew how to farm as well as hunt and fish. They are thought to have been short, slight, dark and wiry, of a physical type still familiar in Britain. They grew wheat, kept cattle, sheep and pigs, made the first pottery in England and constructed the first buildings of any size.

The change from hunting to farming, slowly spreading all over the country, was a decisive step. It meant that most people spent all their lives tied to one place. It meant routine work, grinding physical toil, a less adventurous life, greater comfort but less freedom (and more toothache, incidentally, because of increased consumption of cereals). Man had taken a major initiative in his long experiment in altering his natural environment. In time, as the forests were burned and felled, agriculture created a countryside of farmsteads and villages.

The population swelled. Private property accumulated. An elite priesthood seems to have sprung up, learned in mathematics and astronomy.

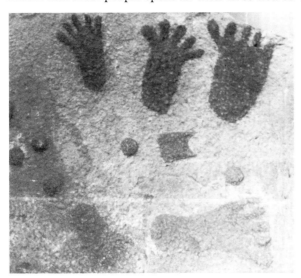

Part of a Bronze Age stone coffin, found near Priddy in Somerset, enigmatically carved with human feet and cup marks, which presumably have a symbolic connection with life after death.

The early hunting peoples gathered wild fruit, such as apples, elderberries and blackberries, to eat and to make medicines and dyes. The early farmers grew corn and a small bean, something like a modern broad bean.

Figure in pine wood, late Bronze Age or early Iron Age, in the Colchester and Essex Museum. It is 19 in (48.5 cm) high. A detachable phallus could be fitted into the hole.

One of the Beaker People's beakers, with a maximum diameter of 8 in (20 cm). They buried these drinking vessels with the dead, and this one was found in the West Kennet Long Barrow in Wiltshire.

Powerful chieftains organized large-scale engineering works – the 'causewayed camps', which may have been used for religious rituals and for markets, and the first 'henge' temples. The dead of the leading families were buried with great toil and reverence in massive stone tombs beneath huge mounds of earth. There were tool factories, and flint mines with shafts as much as 40 ft (12 m) deep, whose products were distributed along a network of tracks and rivers.

The coming of metals
The age of stone tools and weapons drew to a close after 3000 BC, as metal-working began, at first in copper and gold. Then smiths started to alloy copper from Ireland with Cornish tin to make a material tougher than either – bronze. The Bronze Age had dawned, but changes of this kind do not occur all at once. Different groups in England were at different stages of development and probably spoke different languages.

Apparently, the new metal-working technology was introduced by groups of warlike, hard-drinking immigrants from Germany and Holland, who may have been the first Celts in Britain. Successive waves of them came in, it seems, in considerable numbers. They are known to archaeologists as the Beaker People, from the drinking mugs which they buried with their dead under the round barrows that still stand in lines along our hills. They were cattle herders, who had domesticated the horse and who may have brought with them a language from which Welsh and Gaelic are descended.

The period of a thousand years or so after about 2500 BC saw the construction of the bulk of the great stone circles which are the most eerie and impressive legacy of prehistoric England. The rich warlords and cattle barons of Wessex, perhaps led by a dynasty of kings, built the huge stone temples of Avebury and Stonehenge, and profited from trading links with the Mediterranean and the Baltic.

After about 1500 BC the climate changed, becoming colder and wetter. For reasons which are not yet understood, the construction of henges and stone circles and barrows fell away. There are signs of growing tension and hostility, with increased production of weapons – swords, spears, daggers and shields. The earliest hillforts were now constructed for defence, with ramparts of earth and stone topped by wooden palisades.

The age of iron

The next major technological change, from bronze to iron, began roughly about 750 BC. In the last centuries before the arrival of the Roman legions much of the country was divided into Celtic tribal territories, populated by peasant farmers who grew corn and raised cattle and sheep. They fed and supported, and were ruled and protected by, a warrior aristocracy of kings and chieftains. How far this had been a home-grown development, and how far a product of invasion and influence from abroad, is not at all clear, though some groups of Celtic

This small, hermaphroditic fertility figure, carved in ash wood in about 3000 BC, was discovered during excavation of the Bell Track, a prehistoric man-made road in the Somerset marshes, and is now in the Cambridge University Museum of Archaeology.

immigrants certainly shouldered their way in from France. It was a time of much petty warfare, raiding and rustling, with increased production of armaments, the use of cavalry and the introduction of the war chariot. Hillforts grew more numerous, and their defences stronger and more elaborate. Some of them were chieftains' strongholds, to which the

These small chalk drums were found buried with a 5-year-old child at Folkton, North Yorkshire. The owlish eyebrows and eyes may represent the mother goddess to whom the dead child was entrusted.

Beautiful collars, now known as lunulae, were made by Bronze Age craftsmen from Irish gold. They presumably had some link with worship of the moon.

local farmers could retreat when raiders or war-parties were sighted, but some were permanently occupied as fortified villages.

The Celts were head-hunters. The human head had a profound magical mystique for them, and they liked to take their enemies' severed heads back home to hang up at their doors. The Celtic aristocracy were great fighters, drinkers and boasters. They wore cloaks and trousers (perhaps already bearing tartan patterns), with gold armlets and neckbands.

An accomplished Celtic art style developed in England. This bronze-covered wooden bucket of the first century BC was found at Aylesford in Kent. Heads of warriors in crested helmets are carved on it.

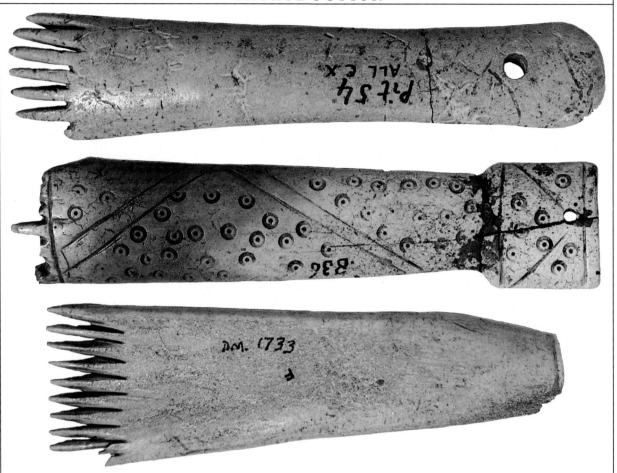

Bone combs were used for weaving in the Iron Age, when Celtic warriors may already have been wearing the forerunners of today's tartan patterns.

They may have been tattooed or they may have put on blue warpaint, and for battle they stiffened their hair into spikes with lime. They were also the patrons of skilled craftsmen – goldsmiths, jewellers, armourers – and of artists with words – the bards. A notable Celtic art style emerged, and religion was dominated by the Druid priesthood.

Late in the second century BC a people the Romans called Belgae, of mixed Celtic and Germanic stock from Belgium and north-eastern France, began raiding across the Channel. Some of them settled in southern England and their leaders carved out kingdoms and lordships for themselves. Caswallon, whose base was in Hertfordshire, seems to have been regarded as high king in the south of England when Julius Caesar launched a punitive expedition to England in 54 BC. Caswallon's descendant Cunobelin (Cymbeline) ruled all the south-east from his capital at Colchester in the following century. In AD 43, however, on the orders of the stuttering Emperor Claudius, the Romans invaded the country they knew as Britannia, and overran England and Wales.

The Roman conquest is accepted as marking the end of the prehistoric period in England. It had lasted an immense length of time. To get an idea of how long, imagine that the whole period from 300,000 BC to the present is compressed into a single week. On this scale 300,000 BC is the first minute of Sunday morning and the present moment, now, is 11.59 on the following Saturday night. The owner of the Swanscombe skull was alive at about 4 o'clock on Monday morning. The Ice Age did not end until today, Saturday, at about 4 o'clock this afternoon. The land bridge to the Continent disappeared at about quarter to 7 this evening and people have been farming since around 8.30. The Roman conquest began. a fraction over an hour ago (and it is just over 5 minutes since the battle of Waterloo).

This beautiful mirror, from Desborough, Northamptonshire, was made not long before the Roman invasion. It has an elegant handle and the back is decorated with a symmetrical curvilinear design.

Reconstruction drawing by Alan Sorrell of the Iron Age village which stood where London Airport is now. The rectangular building in the foreground with ox skulls above the entrance is a temple.

Sites and map references

The most common features of today's landscape left from this vast stretch of time are Bronze Age round barrows, of which there are multitudes. Rarer and more impressive are the stone circles and standing stones, and the long barrows, dolmens and massive stone tombs of the Neolithic period. Located in a past even more remote are the caves where traces of Stone Age hunters have been found. Hillforts of the Iron Age frequently command wonderful views of the surrounding countryside and make delightful picnic places and targets for a walk or a stroll. There is also a distinct pleasure in walking a little way along a track first trodden by human feet thousands of years ago – by prehistoric farmers on the way to a market or a religious ceremony, by axe traders or travelling bronzesmiths — as on the Ridgeway Path or the South Downs Way, Mastiles Lane or stretches of the Cleveland Way. The great majority of prehistoric objects – including human skeletons, axes, weapons and tools, household equipment, jewel-lery and ornaments, chariots and horse harness, boats and coins – are no longer where they were found but have to be contemplated in museums.

This book divides England into nine regions, each with a gazetteer of sites in alphabetical order, though where sites are close together or closely associated they are treated together. A selection of museums of interest is provided and background information about different types of site is given in panels at appropriate points.

National Grid references are supplied for the sites so that they can be found on the Ordnance Survey maps. The reference for Trethevy Quoit in Cornwall, for example, is SX 259688. The letters SX identify the 100 km square in which the site falls. Along the top of the map are numbers at 1 km intervals called eastings, and at the sides are similar numbers called northings. In this case find the easting 25 and move beyond it 0.9 km. Then find the northing 68 and move up a further 0.8 km. The site is where the easting and northing cross.

One of a pair of labyrinths carved on a rock face by a ruined mill in the Rocky Valley in Cornwall, possibly dating from the Bronze Age.

THE WEST COUNTRY
CORNWALL, ISLES OF SCILLY, DEVON, SOMERSET

CORNWALL was the last part of southern Britain to be conquered by the English, a thousand years ago. It has always retained a separate identity and an air of mystery and enchantment, partly due to its wealth of prehistoric sites. The Land's End peninsula is a kind of open-air prehistoric museum, with its stone circles, standing stones and massive 'quoits', or dolmens, the remains of Stone Age tombs. At Chysauster the visitor can see the remains of a village street that is 2000 years old. Cornwall owed much of its prehistoric importance and prosperity to its flourishing trade in tin, which has been known and worked there since the Bronze Age.

There is another concentration of sites on Bodmin Moor and another in Devon, on Dartmoor, with stone circles and mysterious lines of standing stones striding across the moors. Kent's Cavern in Torquay, where Neanderthal families sheltered from the cold, is one of the oldest human homes in Britain. More caves of this kind can be found in the Cheddar Gorge and at Wookey Hole in Somerset, and up on top of the Mendip Hills there is a further concentration of circles and barrows at Priddy. Ham Hill is one of the grandest hillforts in England and another Somerset stronghold, Cadbury Castle, has intriguing Arthurian connections.

Most of central Somerset in prehistoric times was a tangle of swamps flooded by the Bristol Channel. Groups of people established themselves on islands among the marshes, and before 3000 BC were constructing artificial tracks through the wilderness. One of these, the Sweet Track, is the oldest man-made road in Britain.

Museums of interest
Rougemont House Museum, Exeter; Penlee House, Penzance; City Museum & Art Gallery, Plymouth; Somerset County Museum, Taunton; Natural History & Antiquarian Society Museum, Torquay; County Museum & Art Gallery, Truro; Wells Museum.

Cornwall's prehistoric sites help to give it an air of mystery and enchantment. These monoliths near Altarnun are locally called the Nine Stones.

There are 19 stones in the circle of Boscawen-un on the

Land's End peninsula, with a leaning stone in the middle.

PLACES TO VISIT

Blackbury Castle, Devon

SY 188924, *Dept of the Environment*, 3 miles (4.8 km) NW of Seaton, off B3174. This hillfort of about 200 BC has a single rampart of flint and earth, still standing up to 10 ft (3 m) high. The gateway was in the S side, protected by a triangular outer earthwork. There are numerous barrows on the downs to the N.

Bolt Tail, Devon

SX 669396, *National Trust*, W of Marlborough. Iron Age hillfort on the South Devon Coast Path, with views over Bigbury Bay.

Boscawen-un, Cornwall

SW 412274, S of A30, 1 mile (1.6 km) N of St Buryan. Pronounced 'Boscorn-oon', this is a Bronze Age circle of 19 low stones, with a leaning one in the middle and 4 more stones grouped at the NE. The Cornish gorsedd (gathering) of bards is sometimes held here. To the NE, N of A30, is a standing stone, 10 ft (3 m) high, called the **Blind Fiddler** SW 425282 or **Tregonebris Stone**. To the W of Sancreed are the hillfort of **Caer Bran** SW 408291, and the village of **Carn Euny** SW 402289 (*Dept of the Environment*), dating from the first century BC. Though not as impressive as Chysauster, it has a wonderful fogou, or underground passage, about 65 ft (20 m) long, which may have been a secret hidey-hole or a cold storage space.

At the prehistoric village of Carn Euny a long, hidden passage – a fogou – runs underground.

Breen Down, Somerset

ST 300590, *National Trust*, N of Burnham-on-Sea. Bird sanctuary. There is a small promontory fort defended by a bank and ditch, with traces of huts and fields. A temple was built inside the fort in Roman times.

Brent Knoll, Somerset

ST 341510, *National Trust*. The fort on this isolated hill has a single rampart and ditch, and commands a fine view over the Somerset flatlands.

Brentor, Devon

SX 471804. A church dedicated to St Michael is perched on top of this steep, isolated 1100-ft (330-m) hill SW of Lydford, with an earthwork which may have protected an Iron Age hillfort or sacred site. Superb views.

Bury Castle, Somerset

SS 917472, *National Trust*, near Minehead. This impressive Iron Age fort with ramparts 15 ft (4.5 m) high is on a spur above Selworthy, which has claims to be the most beautiful village in England.

Cadbury Castle, Somerset

SY 628252, S of A30, reached by footpath from South Cadbury. Excavated in the 1960s, this large hillfort, its ramparts towering 40 ft (12 m) high in places, may well be the original of Camelot in the Arthurian legends. The hill is 500 ft (150 m) high and commands fine views towards

Trees grow in the defences of Blackbury Castle, a small Iron Age hillfort near Seaton in Devon. An armoury of slingstones was found inside the fort.

Off one end of the Carn Euny fogou is a circular room with a corbelled roof, apparently constructed before the fogou and perhaps as early as the Bronze Age. A food store? A hiding hole? A dungeon?

An aerial photograph of Cadbury Castle which gives a good view of the massive ramparts. In the Dark Ages this hilltop stronghold may have been the headquarters of the legendary King Arthur.

Glastonbury. There was a village on the top in Neolithic and Bronze Age times. The first defences were thrown up about 450 BC and by 100 BC 4 concentric ramparts and ditches protected a small township on the summit, with gates at the SW and NE. At the SE corner of the innermost rampart the skeleton of a young man was found. Thrust head down into a pit, his knees drawn up to his chin, he may have been a human foundation sacrifice, buried in the rampart so that his life energy would strengthen it. In the first century AD the defences were repaired and a temple was built in the middle of the fort. Remains of 20 sacrificed animals were found buried in front of it. In about AD 70 or 80 the fort was stormed, presumably by Roman troops, and the bodies of 30 men, women and children were left strewn in the SW entrance.

In the fifth century AD the stronghold was refortified on a massive scale by a wealthy and powerful chieftain, who may have been the British warleader Arthur, the 'King Arthur' of later legend. A timber hall, 63 ft by 34 ft (19 by 10 m) stood on the summit of the hill and served perhaps as his palace and headquarters. According to legend, Arthur and his men lie sleeping under the hill, awaiting the moment to return to life when Britain needs them. In the eleventh century the hill was reoccupied and refortified yet again, and there was a mint there. The excavations have been covered over and today's visitors are left with the view, the ramparts and their imagination.

Carn Brea, Cornwall

SW 686407, S of A30 between Redruth and Camborne. A medieval castle and a peculiar 1830s monument to one of the local Basset family stand on this dominating hill. Between them are the earthworks of an Iron Age fort and the remains of circular stone huts of the late centuries BC. The stone wall round the castle goes back ultimately to Neolithic times and inside it were found traces of the oldest known village in Britain, with perhaps 100 inhabitants in about 3700 BC.

Carn Gluze, Carn Gloose or Ballowal Barrow, Cornwall

SW 355313, *Dept of the Environment*, to the S of Cape Cornwall, 1 mile (1.6 km) W of St Just, on the Cornwall Coast Path. A dome of earth, still over 10 ft (3 m) high, surmounts and seals off a deep, T-shaped pit, possibly a symbolic entrance to the underworld used for rituals honouring the underworld powers. An extremely unusual site, it has a sinister reputation and is said to be best steered clear of at night.

Castle Dore, Cornwall

SX 103548, on E side of B3269, N of Fowey. Hillfort of about 200 BC with double ramparts and ditches. Centuries later, according to legend, this was the stronghold of King Mark of Cornwall and the setting for the love story of

The unusual site at Carn Gluze was excavated in 1874. It may have been used for the worship of the dark powers of the underworld and a sinister reputation still clings to it.

The Cheddar cliffs, almost 450 ft (137 m) high.

Tristan and Iseult, who were buried here. A memorial stone of the sixth century AD to Drustanus (Tristan?) stands 2 miles (3.2 km) to the S. In 1644 there was fierce fighting at Castle Dore between Cromwell's Parliamentary army and the Royalists, led by Charles I in person.

Chapman Barrows, Devon
SS 695435, on Exmoor, 2 miles (3.2 km) SE of Parracombe. A line of Bronze Age round barrows, up to 9 ft (2.7 m) high, runs E/W. Half a mile (804 m) to the SE is the **Long Stone** SS 705431, a tall standing stone, with more barrows to the S and SE.

Cheddar Gorge, Somerset
Famous for its caves with spectacular rock formations, stalactites and stalagmites. Several of the caves were occupied by small groups of hunters in the Old Stone Age. The most accessible of them is **Gough's Cave** ST 466538, a popular tourist attraction opened up by R.C. Gough in 1893. It was first inhabited between about 12,000 and 8000 BC, and there is some evidence that it was the site of a factory making flint implements. People lived in it again

in the Iron Age and the Roman period. Stone Age weapons and tools are on display in the museum, with animal bones and the skeleton of a young man of 23, who was buried in the cave in about 10,000 BC. He was almost 5 ft 5 in (1.65 m) tall, of slender build, and his leg bones show that he was accustomed to squatting rather than sitting. Examination of his teeth indicated that he had cleaned them regularly. Buried with him was a bone marked like a tally stick, perhaps used for counting animals or for keeping track of the days in a month.

THE HUNTER'S LIFE

For most of his history on earth man has been a hunter and a nomad. Tilling the soil and a settled life in a village or town are comparatively modern innovations. The people who occupied England in the final centuries of the Ice Age – a mere handful by present-day standards, perhaps a few hundred at any one time – lived by hunting, fishing, gathering fruit, berries, nuts and honey, and grubbing for roots. It is a mistake to think of them as brutish ape-men. Though only one in ten of them may have lived to be 40, they looked much like us and had as shrewd a native intelligence as our own. Nor would their life have seemed as dangerous to them as it does to us.

These people lived in small groups, the men doing the hunting and the women gathering food and sewing clothes from animal skins. They ranged over sizeable territories following the game-herds – stalking, driving and trapping bison, reindeer and wild horse. They lived in caves where available (as at Cheddar or Kent's Cavern) or in temporary shelters

A group of nomadic Stone Age hunters have made a temporary camp : artist's reconstruction.

made by digging pits in the ground and covering them over with skins or brushwood supported on poles. They may have made tents of skin. They wore ornaments of seashells and animals' teeth and they created the earliest works of art in England.

With the retreat of the ice and the spread of trees, Middle Stone Age hunters adapted to life in the forests. Still semi-nomadic, they were the first people to domesticate dogs for hunting deer and wild ox. They also invented the bow and arrow. They used dugout canoes, nets and harpoons for fishing. There is evidence that they began to clear the forests with fire and axe, presumably to create fresh pasture for the game they hunted, which means that they started to alter and control their environment, not just live off it. Helped by their dogs, they may have begun to round up and herd deer even before the arrival of the first farmers.

The Cheddar cliffs hem in a winding ravine close to 1 mile (1.6 km) long. Several of its spectacular caves were lived in by Stone Age hunters.

The mushroom-like dolmen called Chun Quoit is what is left of a Neolithic tomb, with a burial chamber walled by 4 uprights and roofed with a huge capstone. Traces of the original covering mound can still be seen.

Chun Quoit, Cornwall

SW 402339, S of Morvah, accessible from B3306 or B3318. The dolmen is like an immense mushroom, with a capstone supported on 4 uprights, the remains of a Neolithic tomb. Nearby to the E is **Chun Castle** SW 405339, a small hillfort of about 200 BC.

Chysauster, Cornwall

SW 47335, *Dept of the Environment*, approached from B3311 at Badger's Cross. This is an extremely interesting place, a village occupied from about 100 BC to AD 200, with houses on either side of the village street. Some of the walls still stand 6 ft (1.8 m) high. Each house was oval or circular, built round an open inner courtyard, with rooms in the 15-ft (4.5-m) thickness of the walls. They may have been roofed with thatch or vaulted over with stone in 'beehive' style, and they had paved floors, covered drains and walled off gardens outside. (A model of the village can be seen in the Penlee House Museum, Penzance.) There is a small fogou to the SE. The villagers probably panned for tin in the nearby stream. The hillfort of **Castle an Dinas** SW 485350, 1 mile (1.6 km) to the E, may have given the villagers a refuge in time of danger. The tower was built in the eighteenth century.

Countisbury Castle, Devon

SS 742493. Fortress on Wind Hill, 1 mile (1.6 km) E of Lynton, with a towering rampart 30 ft (9 m) high. The men of Devon won a great victory over a force of marauding Danes here in 878, annihilating them with a charge downhill from the fort.

Cow Castle, Somerset

SS 795374, 2 miles (3.2 km) SE of Simonsbath. A small, beautiful hillfort on Exmoor, overlooking the River Barle, with a single rampart and ditch.

Duloe, Cornwall

SX 235583, N of Duloe church. A small circle of 8 stones, one of them 9 ft (2.7 m) high.

Dunkery Hill, Somerset

SS 908426, *National Trust*. On the NE slope of the hill are Bronze Age round burial cairns. The largest is **Robin How**, 10 ft (3 m) high.

Exmoor Ridgeway

The scenic road along the Devon–Somerset border, from Mole's Chamber SE to Sandyway Cross, follows a prehistoric track and passes numerous barrows. SW of Mole's Chamber is **Shoulsbury Castle** SS 706391, protected by steep slopes and double ramparts, a prehistoric or possibly a Roman fort.

Glastonbury, Somerset

According to tradition, this much-visited town with its beautiful abbey ruins is the site of the first Christian

The remains of 8 stone houses stand opposite each other across the village street at Chysauster. Hand mills for grinding corn were found here, as well as pottery and domestic refuse.

church in Britain, the place where the Holy Grail lies concealed and the burial place of King Arthur and Queen Guinevere. Some people believe that the terraces on **Glastonbury Tor** ST 513386 are a prehistoric processional way, a spiral path winding up to the summit. Whether this is true is doubtful, but the Tor is certainly likely to have been a sacred place long before the coming of Christianity. At Godney Marsh ST 492409, 1 mile (1.6 km) NW of the modern town, there was a thriving village in 100 BC, of 60 to 70 houses standing on oak piles in the

Another view of Chysauster. The houses had rooms opening off a central courtyard. The hole in the stone in the foreground was the socket for a post which supported the roof.

Topped by the tower of the ruined chapel of St Michael, Glastonbury Tor is a landmark for miles around. It was probably a sacred place long before Christianity came to England.

marshes, and there was another not far away, at Meare. The inhabitants had wheeled vehicles, ploughs, looms and lathes. There is nothing to be seen now except a few humps in the ground, but there are interesting exhibits in the Tribunal at Glastonbury and the Taunton Museum.

Far back in the New Stone Age, before 3000 BC, the people of the marshes constructed wooden trackways connecting settlements in the swamps with each other and with the outside world. The oldest of them, the earliest artificial road yet discovered in Britain, is called the **Sweet Track**, after a peat-cutter named Ray Sweet who discovered it in 1970. It was made of planks fastened down on top of long poles, supported on blocks of peat and held in place with wooden pegs. Tall wooden posts were fixed every few yards to mark the line of the track. A reconstructed section of track has recently been opened to the public, starting at the Godwin Peatworks, 4 miles (6.4 km) W of Glastonbury.

Grimspound, Devon

SX 701809, NE of Postbridge. This is the most impressive of Dartmoor's prehistoric villages, possibly dating from about 1000 BC and surrounded by a wall, 9 ft (2.7 m) thick and originally 6 ft (1.8 m) high. The villagers would have

Stone courses of a hut at Grimspound on Dartmoor. The houses measured about 15 ft (4.5 m) across, with hearths and sleeping benches inside. A central wooden post supported a roof of turf or thatch.

The remains of circular houses, storage huts and cattle pens can be seen inside the encircling wall of the Bronze Age village of Grimspound. The village had its own stream inside the wall.

brought their cattle and sheep inside the walls for safety at night. Inside are a stream and the remains of circular huts, storehouses and cattle pens. The entrance is at the SE with a paved track. The huts had drystone walls 3 ft (1 m) thick and measured up to 15 ft (4.5 m) across, with hearths and sleeping platforms. Some had porches for protection against wind and weather.

Halligye, Cornwall

SW 712238, 4 miles (6.4 km) SE of Helston, N of B3293 at Garras. A torch is needed to explore the fogou here. Fogous are underground passages, found in Cornwall, Brittany, Scotland and Ireland, built by digging a trench, walling it and roofing it over with stone slabs and then scattering earth on top. At Halligye two passages, one of them 54 ft (16 m) long, form a T, and were originally concealed beneath a house which has long since vanished. Across the floor of the main passage is a block of stone which may have been a literal stumbling block. An intruder could easily trip over it in the dark and so give warning of his presence. However, whether fogous were built as refuges from danger or as shrines to underworld powers or – more prosaically – for cold storage purposes is still in some doubt.

HILLFORTS AND EARLY TOWNS

Perched on high ground, hillforts frequently offer commanding views, but the tranquil prospects that please visitors today originally gave lookouts an early view of approaching enemies. The forts date mainly from the last millennium BC, a time of incessant minor warfare, raiding and cattle rustling. Many of them are quite small, and over 50 per cent of them occupy only 3 acres (1.2 ha) or less. These were the eyries of local chieftains and their war-bands, from which they mounted raiding expeditions. Even a small hillfort took much labour to construct. A ditch and rampart would follow a contour line round a hill, or a steep spur or coastal headland would be barricaded off with earthworks

Hillfort ramparts : left *earth piled up in simple glacis topped by palisade ;* centre *palisade acts as revetment for upper rampart and sentry walk ;* right *upper rampart has timber lacing, outside and inside.*

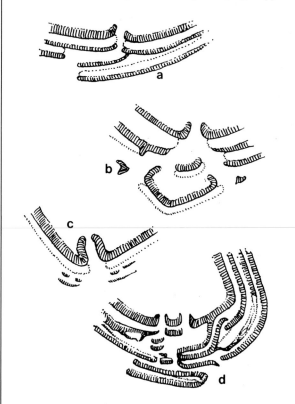

Types of hillfort entrances designed to hinder attackers : a) overlapping ramparts, Hod Hill, Dorset ; b) outwork protecting entrance, Yarnbury, Wiltshire ; c) inturned ramparts, the Wrekin, Shropshire ; d) multiple defences, Maiden Castle, Dorset.

across its neck. The rampart might be faced with timber and reinforced with stone, rearing 50 ft (15 m) or more above the bottom of its ditch and topped with a bristling palisade of sharpened stakes. As time went by, the defences were often strengthened and elaborated with additional ramparts. The entrances, which were the Achilles' heel of a hillfort, were often 'inturned' or shaped like a funnel. They had heavy wooden gates, bridged by a sentry walk, and a row of enemy heads on poles might frown a grim warning to attackers. Outer works could be built to protect the entrance, and complicated approach passages were devised to slow enemies down and expose them to a rain of spears and slingshot from the defenders.

The bigger forts were villages, full of noise and bustle and vigorous life, where today there may be only grass and silence. Inside were the huts of farmers, who tilled the fields below the fort and pastured cattle and sheep. There were also the workshops of smiths, potters and carpenters, with sheds and cattle pens, storage pits for grain and pits for the community's rubbish. These strongholds were the headquarters of powerful chiefs, and the biggest forts of all were centres of administration and trade over large areas. In the south-east, during the last century BC, kings built tribal capitals on low ground. Colchester and Chichester are examples. These large settlements can be considered to be the earliest true towns in Britain.

The fortified township on Ham Hill commands a soaring view over the Fosse Way and the Somerset flatlands. The buildings for miles around are constructed of Ham stone, quarried here.

Ham Hill, Somerset

ST 485166. Looming above the A3088, 1 mile (1.6 km) W of Montacute, is one of the largest and most enjoyable hillforts in England, and probably the only one with a pub inside it. More than 3 miles (4.8 km) of earthworks encompass the hill, best preserved on the NW side. This was a fortified town of the Durotriges, the Celtic people of the area, when the Romans came, and it had been occupied for several centuries before that. There is the site of a Roman villa on the E side and possibly the remains of an amphitheatre in the NE corner. Quarrying for the famous Ham stone since Roman times – buildings for miles around are constructed of it – has created a wilderness of humps and hollows and miniature gorges.

Hembury Fort, Devon

ST 113031, *National Trust*, on the N side of A373, 3 miles (4.8 km) N of Honiton. This splendid hillfort, with marvellous views towards Dartmoor, is defended by ditches and banks originally faced with timber. There were massive timber gateways in the W side and at the NE corner, with cobbled approaches. The defences were probably thrown up by the Dumnonii, the Celtic people of Devon, in the second century BC. Later, in about 50 BC, two banks and ditches were built across the fort E/W and the S end was used as an enclosure for cattle. The hillfort was constructed on top of a far older causewayed camp, made by the farmers and cattle-herders of the area in about 4000 BC.

The Hurlers, Cornwall

SX 258714, *Dept of the Environment*. Three Bronze Age stone circles stand in a line NE/SW on Bodmin Moor, among desolate scenery and ruined tin mines. The builders went to unusual trouble to make sure that the standing stones were all of the same height, and the faces were smoothed by hammering. To the SW are 2 outlying stones, the **Pipers**. Nearby, on a hill to the NE, is the **Rillaton Barrow** SX 260719, about 120 ft (36 m) across and still 8 ft (2.4 m) high. Here, in a stone-lined grave still visible on the E side, was found a single skeleton and, buried with it, the famous Rillaton Gold Cup, made of corrugated sheet gold and now in the British Museum. In the same area of the moor are **Trethevy Quoit** and the weird natural rock formation called the Cheesewring.

Isles of Scilly

There are so many Stone Age tombs on these small islands that they have been identified with the isles of the dead of subsequent Greek and Celtic mythology. Were dead chieftains brought here from the mainland by boat for burial, and did the memory and the awe of it linger on to create the tradition of mysterious islands in the west?

The tombs on St Mary's are of an unusual type, called

The Hurlers are 3 stone circles in a line on Bodmin Moor. The outlying stones to the SW were perhaps placed to mark sunset in early spring and late autumn, and signal the approach of summer and winter.

'entrance graves' and also found in the extreme west of Cornwall, with a stone burial chamber covered over by a circular cairn. Some are in the care of the *Dept of the Environment*. **Bant's Carn** SU 911124 is about 40 ft (12 m) in diameter, with the remains of a passage leading to the entrance. Nearby are a standing stone – the **Long Stone** – and the remains of the circular stone huts of a pre-Roman village. There are two more entrance graves at **Innisidgen** SU 921127 and a restored example at **Porth Hellick Down** SU 929108, near **Giant's Castle** SU 924101, a cliff fort defended by 3 lines of ramparts. There are more tombs on St Martin's, Bryher and the other

The Rillaton Cup was found in this stone-lined grave in the side of Rillaton Barrow. In the background is Stowe Hill and the odd rock formation called the Cheesewring.

The Rillaton Cup stands 3¼ in (8.3 cm) high, of corrugated gold, with a separate handle fastened by rivets. King Edward VII is said to have kept his collar studs in it, but it is now in the British Museum.

islands, and on the little island of Gugh (pronounced 'Hugh') is the **Old Man of Gugh**, a standing stone 9 ft (2.7 m) tall.

Kent's Cavern, Devon

SX 934641, in Ilsham Road, Torquay. A famous tourist attraction, with its beautiful caves, galleries and ice formations, this is one of the oldest homes in Britain, occupied down to the end of the Ice Age by hunters. They left behind them tools of flint, bone and antler, including harpoons and a needle. Some hand axes found here are thought to be 300,000 years old or even more. The caves were also occupied from time to time by animals – mammoth, woolly rhino, cave bear, lion, hyena. The skull of a cave bear is on show, but the principal display of finds, including a human skull, can be seen at the Torquay Natural History Society Museum.

Kes Tor, Devon

SX 665867, on Dartmoor, 2 miles (3.2 km) SW of Chagford. On the N slopes of the Tor are the remains of about 25 stone huts of an Iron Age village. Stones mark the boundaries of fields and there are two drove roads, on either side of the Batworthy Road. The **Round Pound**, an oval enclosure 110 ft (33 m) across, had a round hut at the centre with an iron-smelting furnace in it. A roof of turf or thatch was supported on a ring of posts. Here the smith lived and worked apart, in about 400 BC, to keep the mysteries of his craft safe from prying eyes and preserve his magical mystique. To the NW, on Gidleigh Common, is the **Scorhill Circle** SX 655874, one of the finest on the moor, with more than 20 stones standing, the tallest over 8 ft (2.4 m) high.

SW of Kes Tor, on **Shovel Down** SX 660860, are stone rows leading to burial cairns and a 10-ft (3-m) monolith, the **Longstone**. A stone avenue may originally have led from the Scorhill Circle to the **Fernworthy Circle** SX 655841 and on to **Grey Wethers** SX 638832, two circles close together which were restored in the nineteenth century. There are more stone rows on Chagford Common and further S at Challacombe.

One of the Stone Age 'carns' at Innisidgen, Isles of Scilly. The rectangular burial chamber is roofed over by 5 stone blocks and surrounded by a mound.

The Longstone on Shovel Down, Dartmoor, in an area of stone rows and prehistoric burials.

Lanyon Quoit, Cornwall

SW 430337, *National Trust*. This famous dolmen, rebuilt in 1824, stands like a giant's granite table beside the road between Madron and Morvah. A few traces can be seen of the mound which originally covered the burial chamber.

Men-an-Tol, Cornwall

SW 427349. To the N of Lanyon Quoit and the Madron–Morvah road is one of the most famous objects in Cornwall, a large circular stone with a hole carefully pierced through its middle, standing between 2 upright stones. Down into the eighteenth century children were passed through the hole to cure them of rickets and skin diseases. Symbolically, the procedure may have meant that they 'died' and were healthily restored to life again, for the stone may originally have been the entrance to a burial chamber. To the N are the remains of the Nine Maidens stone circle.

Merrivale, Devon

SX 553746, *Dept of the Environment*, on Dartmoor, just to the S of B3357, near the granite quarries. There are hut circles here and the remains of a Bronze Age sacred complex. Two stone avenues run E/W, one with a barrow in it and each blocked by a stone at the E end. To the W is another barrow and a stone row. To the E of this row is a large stone cist with a split cover slab, and to the S is a stone circle, about 60 ft (18 m) in diameter, with an outlier to the S.

The Merry Maidens or Stone Dance, Cornwall

SW 433245. On the S side of B3315, W of Boleigh, 19 stones about 4 ft (1.2 m) high form a perfect circle some 60 ft (18 m) across. On the other side of the road, a little to the NE, are two standing stones of somewhat sinister aspect called the **Pipers**. One is 15 ft (4.5 m) high and the other is 13½ ft (4 m) high. Another outlier, the **Fiddler**, is to the W of the circle. The legend is that the maidens and the musicians were turned to stone for dancing on a Sunday. To the W along B3315 is the **Tregiffian Round Barrow** SW 430245 (*Dept of the Environment*) with a burial chamber on the S side.

The Merry Maidens are supposed to have been turned to stone as a punishment for dancing on a Sunday. The circle is also known as the Stone Dance.

Lanyon Quoit collapsed and was rebuilt early in the nineteenth century, but to only half its previous height. The capstone is about 18 ft (5.4 m) long by 9 ft (2.7 m) broad.

The Nine Maidens, Cornwall

SW 937676, 3 miles (4.8 km) NE of St Columb Major, on E side of A39. A mysterious line of standing stones stretches for 100 yards or so (about 90 m) in a NE/SW alignment.

Priddy, Somerset

There is a legend that Jesus spent part of his boyhood in this Mendips village, in a prehistoric sacred area bristling with Bronze Age antiquities, including over 100 barrows. The caves in the nearby Ebbor Gorge were used by Stone Age hunters. The mysterious **Priddy Circles** ST 540350 are 4 henges in a N/S line ¾ mile (1.2 km) long. Each is about 600 ft (182 m) in diameter, marked off by a bank and a ditch which, unusually, is outside the bank. The old Roman road runs between them. To the S are **Ashen Hill Barrows** ST 538521, 8 large bowl barrows in an E/W line. To the S again, about 1 mile (1.6 km) NE of Priddy itself, are **Priddy Nine Barrows** ST 538516, up to 80 ft (24 m) across and 10 ft (3 m) high. In a field to the N of the B3134 road, near Pool Farm ST 537541, ¾ mile NW of the Castle of Comfort Inn, is a copy of an enigmatic Bronze Age stone cist, decorated with carvings of human feet, cup marks and a horned symbol. The original, now in the City Museum, Bristol, contained the cremated remains of an adult and child, and was covered by a round barrow. This

The stone-lined grave in the Tregiffian Round Barrow, near the Merry Maidens stone circle, among the cluster of prehistoric sites on the Land's End peninsula.

was evidently a venerated area, where chiefs or priests and their families were buried.

Rocky Valley, Cornwall

SX 073893. A beautiful valley runs from B3263 down to the coast near Bossiney. On the way, on a rock face, are two small carvings of labyrinths, of uncertain date.

The famous Men-an-Tol, or 'stone of the hole', stands between 2 uprights. It may originally have been

a 'porthole' entrance to a Neolithic burial chamber, and was long believed to have magical powers.

The Rumps cliff fort. The landward side is defended by triple ramparts and ditches. There was a flourishing settlement here in the first century BC, with trading contacts with France.

Rough Tor, Cornwall

SX 145800, *National Trust*. Rough (pronounced to rhyme with cow) Tor is the second highest point on Bodmin Moor (Brown Willy is the highest). At the summit are impressive rock piles, gingerly balanced on top of each other, and the remains of a small hillfort. On the slope between the Tor and the car park are the foundations of circular stone huts and the stone walls of fields and cattle pens of about 1000 BC. To the S and SW are more hut circles and the stone circles of **Stannon** SX 126800, **Fernacre** SX 144800 and **Leaze** SX 137773.

The Rumps, Cornwall

SW 934810, *National Trust*. This cliff fort on Rumps Point, N of Pentire, on the Cornwall Coast Path, commands splendid views. Triple ramparts and deep ditches of the first century BC protected a village here. The foundations of huts belonging to the settlement were found inside the fortifications along with bones of the villagers' cows, sheep and pigs.

The Spinster's Rock dolmen, near Drewsteignton, fell down in 1862 and was re-erected. Three uprights support a massive capstone.

Tarr Steps. This clapper bridge over the River Barle on Exmoor consists of 17 stone slabs weighing up to 5 tons each. The bridge has been frequently rebuilt, but may go back to prehistoric times.

Spinster's Rock, Devon

SX 700908, just to the E of A382, S of Whiddon Down. A local story says that three spinsters put this dolmen up one day before breakfast. It has a capstone and 3 uprights.

Stripple Stones, Cornwall

SX 144752. A stone circle stands on the slope of Hawkstor to the N of the A30, with one fallen stone near the centre. The date is probably late Neolithic or early Bronze Age. To the W, near the minor road to Bradford, is another circle, the **Trippet Stones** or **Dancing Stones.**

Tarr Steps, Somerset

SS 868321. A celebrated bridge on the River Barle on Exmoor, SW of Winsford Hill. The bridge is 180 ft (55 m) long, with stone slabs weighing up to 5 tons each. It may have been built in prehistoric times originally, though undoubtedly it has been repaired and rebuilt frequently since then. According to legend, the Devil constructed it in a single night to win a bet with a giant.

To the NE, just E of Spire Cross, is the **Caratacus Stone** SS 889335 (*National Trust*). Inscribed CARATACI NEPUS, 'nephew of Caradoc', it apparently commemorates a relative of the British chief who fiercely resisted the Roman invasion. Also on Winsford Hill are the **Wambarrows** SS 876343, to the N of B3223: 3 round barrows with a fourth to the SE.

Trencrom, Cornwall

SW 518362, *National Trust*. Small hillfort W of Lelant with a single rampart and traces of huts inside. Fine views.

Treryn Dinas or Treen Dinas, Cornwall

SW 397222, *National Trust*. Cliff fort on a headland S of Treen, with marvellous coastal scenery and a natural 65-ton rocking stone, the Logan Rock. In 1824 it was thrown down by an impetuous naval lieutenant, named Goldsmith, with a party of sailors. Public outcry forced him to replace it at his own expense, but it has never rocked quite so well since.

Trencrom Hill, looking towards St Michael's Mount with its fairytale castle. In prehistoric times the Mount was an important depot in the Cornish tin trade. Tin was collected there for buyers from the Continent.

Trethevy Quoit, Cornwall

SX 259688, *Dept of the Environment*. This massive and spectacular dolmen stands on Bodmin Moor, NE of St Cleer and not far from the **Hurlers**. It is all that remains of a Neolithic tomb, originally covered by a mound. A capstone over 11 ft (3 m) long leans at an angle on top of 6 uprights, and the burial chamber beneath is divided in two by a cross stone. Trethevy means 'place of the grave'.

Trevelgue Head, Cornwall

SX 827630, on the Cornwall Coast Path, NE of Newquay on Porth Island, reached from B3276. A tremendous cliff fort guards a harbour which was used for the tin trade in the third century BC. No fewer than 6 ramparts and ditches protect the headland, as does the sea itself at high tide. There was a bronze smelting centre here which manufactured horse trappings, some of which were found inside the fort.

Trowlesworthy Warren, Devon

SX 574645, *National Trust*, on Dartmoor, accessible on foot from Cadover Bridge. The remains of numerous huts and defensive walls, probably of Bronze Age date, can be seen here, with a stone circle and 2 stone rows. To the N, across the River Plym, is **Legis Tor** SX 570654, with traces of huts and cattle enclosures, a stone circle to the W and barrows and stone rows to the N.

Veryan, Cornwall

SX 913387, ½ mile (804 m) S of Veryan village. An enormous Bronze Age round barrow, one of the biggest in England. Close to 350 ft (106 m) across, it stands 15 ft (4.5 m) high.

The round barrow at Veryan in Cornwall is one of the largest in England and was presumably the final resting place of a powerful chieftain or a dynasty of chiefs.

Trethevy Quoit on Bodmin Moor is one of the most impressive and accessible of the Cornish dolmens. The tallest uprights are close to 15 ft (4.5 m) high.

Wookey Hole, Somerset

ST 532479. The spectacular cave system through which the River Axe flows, with its stalactites and stalagmites and the sinister rock formation called the Witch of Wookey, is now run by Madame Tussaud's and attracts many visitors. It was inhabited in the late centuries BC and there is a museum of Celtic and Roman finds, animal bones, jewellery and pottery. The smaller cave known as the **Hyena Den**, close by, was occupied sporadically much earlier, from about 35,000 BC, by groups of hunters and also by generations of hyenas. Flint and bone implements, the remains of hearths and vast numbers of animal bones were found here in the 1850s and '60s.

Zennor Quoit, Cornwall

SW 469380, on the moors SE of Zennor village. The dolmen has a huge capstone, 18 ft (5.4 m) long and weighing as much as 12 tons – one of the largest in England. Cremated bones, flints and Neolithic pottery were found in the burial chamber beneath.

The most visited and admired prehistoric monument in England, Stonehenge represents an astonishing feat of construction and organization.

THE SOUTH
WILTSHIRE, DORSET, HAMPSHIRE, ISLE OF WIGHT

THIS is archaeologically the richest area in England, full of 'plums'. Its rolling chalk uplands of Salisbury Plain, the Marlborough Downs, the Dorset hills and the Hampshire Downs were forested in prehistoric times. They were cleared by the Neolithic farmers and their grazing cattle, and by about 3000 BC the landscape was beginning to look not unlike it does today. By about 2000 BC the area had a substantial population, dominated by a wealthy and powerful aristocracy of cattle ranchers, who controlled trade routes to the Continent in one direction and to Ireland in the other. Allied with them was an elite priesthood, skilled in astronomy and mathematics. There may have been a dynasty of kings or priest-kings, based at Durrington Walls near Stonehenge.

It was this society, sometimes called the Wessex culture, which built the great sacred complexes of Stonehenge and Avebury, with their towering monoliths, stone circles and avenues, and which spent perhaps 50 years throwing up the man-made mountain of Silbury Hill. Another, previously unknown complex, of about 2000 BC, was discovered in 1982 to the east of Winchester, on the site of a new motorway interchange. The dead of the leading families were buried in hundreds of barrows close to these centres and within their sacred and magical aura – an aura which can still be sensed today, especially at Avebury. For reasons now unknown, the Wessex culture faded away in about 1500 BC, but it has left its monuments behind.

Though Stonehenge and Avebury take pride of place, there are many other sites of exceptional interest. Fyfield Down in Wiltshire has been described as the nearest thing to a prehistoric landscape still to be seen in southern England. Dorset has the famous Cerne Abbas Giant, brandishing his club on his hillside, as well as the Christianized henge at Knowlton, several small circles, the longest cursus in the world and what is perhaps the most impressive hillfort in all England – Maiden Castle, near Dorchester, which the Romans took by storm against fierce resistance. Other impressive Dorset and Hampshire hillforts include Hambledon Hill, Hod Hill, Danebury Ring and Hengistbury Head.

Museums of interest
Alexander Keiller Museum, Avebury; Red House Museum, Christchurch; Wiltshire Archaeological Society Museum, Devizes; Dorset County Museum, Dorchester; Salisbury & South Wiltshire Museum, Salisbury.

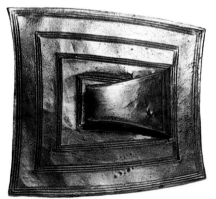

A great chieftain of the Wessex culture was buried in the Bush Barrow, an 11-ft (3.3-m) bowl barrow on Normanton Down, with treasures which included this golden belt fastening.

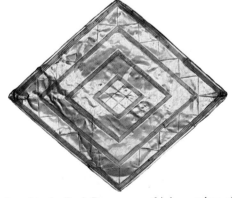

Also found in the Bush Barrow was this breastplate of gold, measuring $7\frac{1}{2} \times 6\frac{1}{4}$ in (18.4 × 15.9 cm), made by a master craftsman in about 2000 BC. The finds from the barrow are in the Devizes Museum.

PLACES TO VISIT

Abbotsbury, Dorset

There is a cluster of prehistoric sites on the downland above Abbotsbury and Portisham, including numerous barrows. Many can be seen from the Hardy Monument. **Abbotsbury Castle** SY 555866, 1 mile (1.6 km) NW of Abbotsbury and N of B3517, is a small hillfort looking out over Chesil Bank, with a round barrow inside and traces of huts and walls. The small rectangular enclosure at the W end may have been a Roman signal station. About 2 miles (3.2 km) NE of Abbotsbury is the **Grey Mare and her Colts** SY 584871, reached by a path from the road from Abbotsbury to Winterbourne St Martin. This Neolithic long barrow is 75 ft (22 m) long and has the remains of a stone burial chamber at the SE end. About a mile to the E is another, restored, Neolithic tomb called the **Hell Stone** SY 605867.

To the NW of the Grey Mare is the **Kingston Russell Stone Circle** SY 577878 (*Dept of the Environment*), 1 mile SW of Little Bredy, with 18 stones, all fallen, in an oval 80 ft (24 m) across. Nearby, at the foot of Crow Hill,

Adam in the foreground, with Eve in the distance. These stones are all that is left of an avenue approaching Avebury from the W, destroyed in the eighteenth century.

is the Valley of Stones SY 597877, with blocks of stone left behind by an Ice Age glacier. This is the probable source of the sarsens and stone slabs used in the circles and tombs of this area. Celtic fields and lynchets can be seen on the hillsides.

The main circle at Avebury, the biggest in Britain, has small circles inside it and is approached along an avenue of stones from the SE.

Avebury from the air. Much of the village is inside the prehistoric sanctuary, which is the largest of its kind in Europe and covers an area more than 13 times the size of Stonehenge.

Avebury, Wiltshire

SU 103700, *Dept of the Environment* and *National Trust*. This riveting place is the biggest sanctuary of its kind in Europe and despite the toll of the centuries is vastly impressive. It covers an area large enough to house half a dozen cathedrals, approaching 30 acres (12 ha), with much of Avebury village inside it and the church just outside. People probably came here from considerable distances to attend spectacular religious ceremonies, perhaps for as much as a thousand years from about 2600 to 1600 BC (a period as long as from our own day back to before the Norman conquest).

Enormous effort was required to build Avebury and it was planned to a complex geometry. It consists essentially of two adjoining stone circles, surrounded by an outer circle, which is surrounded by a ditch, which is surrounded by a bank. The bank very likely served as a grandstand for spectators. It is about ¾ mile (1.2 km) long, 75 ft (22.5 m) thick at the base, and stood perhaps 55 ft (16.5 m) above the bottom of its ditch. It contained 200,000 tons of chalk, now grassed over but in its heyday a bright, glimmering white. The ditch inside it was originally 30 ft (9 m) deep and 15 ft (4.5 m) wide at the bottom. Although it has silted up, it is a sobering experience to stand in it, look up at the bank and remember that the whole thing was dug by men using deer antlers for picks and the shoulder blades of oxen for shovels.

There were 4 entrances through the bank and ditch, at the 4 compass points. Inside the ditch the outer stone circle, the largest in Britain, comprised about 100 hulking monoliths (31 still standing), weighing 40 tons or more each, dragged and manhandled from the downland to the east, where sarsens or 'grey wethers' can still be seen, humped on the turf. Inside this main circle are the remains of the 2 inner ones, each more than 300 ft (90 m) across. Inside the N circle 3 large stones formed a 'cove', a box-shaped setting facing NE. Inside the S circle, just off centre, was a single stone which stood 21 ft (6.3 m) tall, and outside to the S stood a solitary stone with a hole through it. Well into the nineteenth century people used to dance round a maypole in the S circle, perhaps unconsciously echoing dances and rituals performed there thousands of years before.

From the S entrance of the complex a curving stone

The West Kennet Long Barrow was restored in the 1950s. One of the largest in England, it was used for many centuries after about 3400 BC. It is orientated E/W with the burial chambers at the E end.

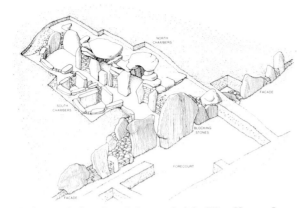

An isometric drawing of the E end of the West Kennet Long Barrow shows the blocking stones and the central corridor, off which the burial chambers open.

avenue, presumably for processions of priests, can be seen running SE (beside B4003). The avenue is 50 ft (15 m) wide and originally had about 100 pairs of stones, arranged with a slender upright facing a diamond-shaped one, possibly as symbols of male and female. The avenue ran for 1½ miles (2.4 km) to the site now known as the **Sanctuary** SU 119679 (*Dept of the Environment*) on Overton Hill, near the River Kennet, just S of the A4 road. There is little to be seen there now, but a large wooden roundhouse once stood at this spot, perhaps the place where the priests lived, as in a college or monastery. To the N are some imposing round barrows. To the N of the Beckhampton crossroads are two standing stones, **Adam and Eve** SU 089693, which once were part of another stone avenue, leading to the W entrance to Avebury.

The displays in Avebury Museum include a skeleton under the floorboards and finds from the causewayed camp on **Windmill Hill** SU 086714 (*Dept of the Environment and National Trust*), a mile or so (1.6 km) to the NW. Not much is visible on the hill any longer, but the camp was encircled by 3 ditches, crossed by numerous causeways and enclosing 21 acres (8.5 ha). It was constructed about 3400 BC. Human skulls, animal bones and implements were found in the ditches. The camp was probably a religious and trading centre in this area before the Avebury sanctuary was built. There are barrows of a later period inside it and nearby.

Many barrows cluster round Avebury, notably the impressive **West Kennet Long Barrow** SU 104677 (*Dept of the Environment*) in a field just S of A4. This mound of chalk and turf, 330 ft (100 m) long, was piled up over large boulders at about the time when the Windmill Hill Camp was constructed. Inside, 5 burial chambers open off a long passage running from the entrance at the E end. The tomb was used over many centuries and 50 or more people were buried in it, including a dozen children. Most of them had suffered from arthritis. One elderly man had died with an arrow in his throat. Some of the skulls

were missing. Were they among those found in the Windmill Hill ditches? Many of the bodies were disarticulated when put in the tomb. They had been exposed somewhere to decompose, perhaps on Windmill Hill, for a long time before burial. Grooves and polished areas can be seen inside the tomb at spots where the workmen who built it sharpened their axes. There is an example on the N face of the stone between the SW burial chamber and the long passage. Outside, the entrance at the E is closed by a façade of massive upright stones, the largest 12 ft (3.6 m) tall. The tomb was restored in the 1950s.

To the E is the **Ridgeway Path**, running N past the Sanctuary and over Avebury Down. Crossing it is the Roman road from London to Bath, which dodges round the cone of **Silbury Hill** SU 100685 (*Dept of the Environment*), looming beside the A4. It is not a natural hill but a skilfully constructed man-made one, standing 130 ft (39 m) high on a base covering over 5 acres (2 ha) and containing close to 9 million cubic feet (254,700 cubic metres) of chalk. It was built in steps like a giant wedding cake and then smoothed over. A labour force of 500 toiling away all year round would have taken 15 years to build the hill. More likely it took 50 years to complete, with people working on it only in the autumn after getting the harvest in. It belongs to the same period as the Avebury Sanctuary and presumably formed part of the sacred complex. Was it the grandiose tomb of the master-architect of Avebury? Perhaps, although excavations have revealed no sign

A view inside the barrow. The burial crypts and the central passage were constructed of boulders from the downs nearby. Over this a mound of chalk was heaped up.

At the end of its long life, the West Kennet barrow was filled with chalk rubble and

closed off at the E end. The enormous central blocking stone stands 12 ft (3.6 m) high.

whatever that anyone was buried in it. Nobody knows what it was for, though it has been calculated that building it consumed a proportion of the gross national product of the time comparable to that expended by the United States of America on its entire space programme.

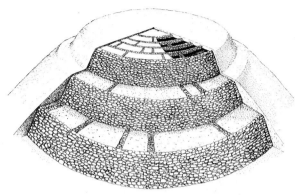

The diagram shows how Silbury Hill was constructed, in revetted tiers like a giant wedding cake, before being covered over with a mound of earth.

Silbury Hill was the first site in Britain to be officially classified and protected as an ancient monument, in 1883. The mystery of why it was built is still unsolved.

TEMPLES OF STONE

There are hundreds of henges and stone circles in England. They range in date over the 2000 years after about 3500 BC, so they had a long life of usefulness and importance. Some have burials inside them. Some form part of complexes of circles, stone avenues and standing stones. Some are circular, others are flattened, oval or egg-shaped – by design, for they were skilfully laid out. Many of them seem to have been built using a common unit of measurement, the 'megalithic yard' (2.72 ft/82 cm). Many of them appear to incorporate a surprisingly sophisticated knowledge of astronomy, with the circle and its outlying stones providing sight-lines not only to the rising and setting of the sun at the seasonal turning points of the year, but to the far more complicated courses of the moon.

Alignments of this kind presumably served practical, religious and magical purposes. A circle was a stone calendar, useful for planning and regulating the seasonal operations of a farming community, but also for determining the correct timing of rituals linked with the cycle of the year and regarded as essential to life, health and prosperity. It was a magic circle separated from the surrounding every-day world, a zone where sacred power was concentrated. It was the temple of a religion in which the great powers of sky and earth were probably the objects of worship and the fertility of fields, herds and women probably the main preoccupation of the worshippers. For the priests and wise men who designed it, the circle and its outliers may also have been a representation in stone of the order of the universe as they understood it, and so magically a way of preserving the order of life on earth.

Judging from surviving rituals and customs on May Day and Hallowe'en, the rites performed at stone circles involved dancing in animal masks and costumes, mimicry of beasts such as the bull and the stag, and leaping over and through fires. There may have been darker rites as well, and perhaps sacrifices. It is significant that so many legends about the circles connect them with dancing, merry-making and, from a Christian point of view, evil – such as the oft repeated story that a circle is a ring of women who were turned to stone for dancing or revelling on a Sunday. Centuries old now, the stones stand on moor and heath, grey and weathered relics of a vanished system of science and belief.

The elegant hour-glass shape of the fort on Beacon Hill, its ramparts following the contour lines. There may have been an earlier causewayed camp on the hill.

Badbury Rings, Dorset

ST 964030, a popular beauty spot 3 miles (4.8 km) NW of Wimborne Minster, N of B3082. The hillfort has double ramparts and a smaller, perhaps later, bank outside. Two Roman roads cross here – the Ackland Dyke from Dorchester to Old Sarum, and the road from Poole to Bath.

Barbury Castle, Wiltshire

SU 149763, 5 miles (8 km) S of Swindon, on the **Ridgeway Path**. An impressively formidable hillfort, where jewellery and coins have been found. It is now a country park.

To the NE, near Badbury, is another imposing hillfort, **Liddington Castle** SU 209797, which according to one theory is the site of the battle of Mount Badon, where the Britons led by Arthur routed the Saxons. Both places were favourite haunts of Richard Jefferies, the nineteenth-century naturalist and author of *Bevis*.

Beacon Hill, Hampshire

SU 458573, in a country park on A34 2 miles (3.2 km) N of Litchfield. The steep hill is topped by a fort of about 100 BC, shaped like an hour-glass, with the entrance on the S, commanding fine views. There are traces of huts and storage pits inside. In the SW corner is the fenced off grave of Lord Carnarvon, who discovered the tomb of Pharaoh Tutankhamun in Egypt in 1922 and died soon after, supposedly struck by 'the mummy's curse'. On the other side of A34 is **Ladle Hill** SU 478568, with round barrows and an unfinished hillfort of about 100 BC. Parts of the ditch were dug and the spoil thrown up to build a rampart, but for some unknown reason the work was abandoned. About 1 mile (1.6 km) to the S on A34 are the **Seven Barrows** SU 463555, Bronze Age round barrows in a N/S line, damaged by ploughing.

Bratton Camp, Wiltshire

ST 900516, *Dept of the Environment*, 2 miles (3.2 km) E of Westbury, off B3098. The hillfort has a long barrow inside and splendid views. Below, on the side of the hill, is a white horse, recut in 1778. How old the earlier horse was is not known, but it may have been pre-Roman.

Breamore, Hampshire

To the NW of the village is the miz-maze on Breamore Down, SU 131208. Cut in turf, it is about 90 ft (27 m) wide. It goes back at least to medieval times and perhaps much earlier, to prehistoric ritual dances. To the S is a long barrow.

Aerial view of Badbury Rings hillfort, now wooded, encircled by 3 sets of banks. It was used as a sighting point by Roman road-builders and 2 Roman roads cross here.

The medieval miz-maze (turf maze) on Breamore Down may have its origin in prehistoric ritual dances. The paths lead to a low mound in the centre.

The Cerne Giant strides across Giant Hill near Cerne Abbas. Above his head is the Trendle or Frying Pan, a rectangular earthwork which may have contained a temple.

The Cerne Giant's outstretched left hand, cut into the chalk. He stands 180 ft (55 m) high and his colossal studded club is 120 ft (36 m) long. His date may be Roman or pre-Roman.

Butser Hill, Hampshire

SU 712201, in a country park, to the W of A3, 3 miles (4.8 km) SW of Petersfield. The earthworks on the hill may be unfinished defences. On the SE slopes are 'Celtic' fields with lynchets. The Butser Ancient Farm Project is a reconstruction of a working farm of about 300 BC, with the methods, crops and animals as much in period as possible. The farm's demonstration area, which is open to the public, is next to the Country Park Centre on A3. To the SE of Petersfield there is a fine collection of barrows scattered about the golf course on **Petersfield Heath** SU 758232.

The Cerne Giant, Dorset

ST 667016, *National Trust*. A celebrated and rampant male figure, 180 ft (55 m) high and wielding an immense club 120 ft (36 m) long, is cut in the turf of Giant Hill to the N of Cerne Abbas. He may be a figure of Hercules, carved in Roman times, or is possibly older, the deity of a Celtic fertility cult. Certainly he has a long-established connection with fertility. Above his head is a small earthwork, called the **Trendle** or the **Frying Pan**, which may have been a temple. A maypole was erected there for many centuries and people danced around it to promote fertility. It is said that even today childless couples still pay visits to the Giant.

Recreation of a house of about 300 BC at the Butser Ancient Farm Project, which as far as possible uses the crops, livestock and farming techniques of the Iron Age.

Clearbury Ring, Wiltshire

SU 152244. Hillfort on an isolated, tree-clad hill S of Salisbury. To the S are stretches of **Grim's Ditch**, an earthwork of about 100 BC, which may have enclosed a large cattle ranch.

Cley Hill, Wiltshire

ST 839449, *National Trust*, 3 miles (4.8 km) W of Warminster, N of A362. A striking, isolated hill 800 ft (246 m) high: on top is an Iron Age fort with 2 round barrows inside and traces of huts on the NW side.

Danebury Ring, Hampshire

SU 323377, 3 miles (4.8 km) NW of Stockbridge. This magnificent hillfort has an inner rampart still standing, up to 16 ft (4.8 m) high and almost 60 ft (18 m) thick at the base. There appears to have been a shrine on the hill in about 1000 BC and the bones of dismembered dogs have been found in ritual pits, where they were buried beneath tall wooden posts. The first defences were constructed in the fifth century BC and were later strengthened and elaborated. Inside the fort there was a thriving village, neatly laid out, with huts arranged in streets on the S side, and the storage area to the N. A little to the N of the fort are 3 long barrows. Not far away, on **Stockbridge Down** SU 375348 (*National Trust*), 1 mile (1.6 km) E of Stockbridge, N of A272, are 'Celtic' fields and small barrows. To the NW is **Woolbury Ring** SU 381353, a large hillfort with a single ditch and bank, and fine views to the Isle of Wight.

Eggardon Hill, Dorset

SY 541947, 2 miles (3.20 km) SE of Powerstock. A tremendous Iron Age hillfort with triple ramparts, entrances at the E and NW and splendid views: traces of huts and storage pits inside, and 2 barrows.

Cley Hill, which some people believe to have a magnetic attraction for flying saucers.

The complex of earthworks at Hambledon Hill in Dorset, the site of a thriving Celtic settlement when the Romans arrived. There is a Neolithic long barrow on the hill where the banks are close together, and the remains of a causewayed camp outside the fort.

Enford, Wiltshire

SU 129516, on the hillside above A345, 1 mile (1.6 km) W of Enford. The Bronze Age bowl barrow here is thought to be the biggest bowl barrow in southern England. It stands 17 ft (5 m) high and is 150 ft (45 m) across.

Figsbury Ring, Wiltshire

SU 188338, *National Trust*, 4 miles (6.4 km) NE of Salisbury, N of A30. Hillfort of about 400 BC, with fine views over Salisbury. It is unusual in having an internal ditch, possibly remaining from an older henge.

Fyfield Down, Wiltshire

SU 142710, 2 miles (3.2 km) E of Avebury. Now a nature reserve, this is the closest thing to a prehistoric landscape left in the south of England. The rectangular Celtic fields with banks and tracks between them date from about 700 BC. The sarsens sprawled on the downland are the first cousins of those used to build Avebury and Stonehenge.

Giant's Grave, Wiltshire

SU 189583. Long barrow of about 3500 BC, 315 ft (29 m) long and 7 ft (2.1 m) high, on a hill above Pewsey to the SE, near the Pewsey White Horse.

Hambledon Hill, Dorset

ST 845125, 1 mile (1.6 km) E of Child Okeford. The impressive fort on this 600-ft (180-m) hill, with tremendous double earthworks and over 200 hut platforms inside, was presumably a township of the Durotriges, the Celtic people who were here when the Romans came. The main entrances are at the SW and NE, with bastions. There are 2 long barrows on the hill, one of them inside the fort. Outside the fort to the SE are faint traces of a far older causewayed camp of about 3500 BC. In its ditches and pits were found many human skulls, with animal bones, flint axes, arrowheads and pottery.

Surprisingly close by to the s is **Hod Hill** ST 857106, above the River Stour. Another hillfort and Durotriges

The fort on Hod Hill is close to the one on Hambledon Hill and may have had the same architect. The area separated off in one corner was a Roman fort.

settlement, it was occupied from about 400 BC. There are numerous hut circles in the SE area. The stronghold was taken by the Roman army in AD 44 and they built a fort in the NW corner, which was occupied for 10 years or so by a garrison of 850 men.

Hengistbury Head, Dorset

SZ 164910. This headland s of Christchurch Harbour is popular with visitors. There are 13 Bronze Age round barrows on it, and it was later occupied from about 500 BC until Roman times. Twin ramparts defended a thriving port, trading with Normandy and Brittany and importing wine from Italy. There was probably a mint here and more than 3000 coins have been discovered. Gold coins and bracelets have also been picked up on the beach below the headland from time to time.

Isle of Wight

The island was part of the mainland until the Ice Age glaciers melted and the sea level rose. Its principal prehistoric antiquities are burials, the long barrows of the Neolithic farmers who cleared the forest and the round barrows of their Bronze Age successors.

There are numerous round barrows and 1 long barrow on **Afton Down** SZ 352857, 1 mile (1.6 km) SE of Freshwater, on the golf course. **Chollerton Down**

THE CAUSEWAYED CAMPS: A MYSTERY

More than 40 'causewayed camps' have been discovered in the south of England and the Midlands. They were constructed by the early Neolithic farmers between about 4000 and 3300 BC, and they are circular or oval enclosures, usually on hilltops, surrounded by up to four concentric banks and ditches. Numerous causeways, made by simply leaving sections of ditch undug, lead across the ditches to entrance gaps in the banks.

These enclosures are an archaeological puzzle. They were not permanent settlements. They do not seem to have been fortresses or cattle corrals. Building them required labour on a scale beyond the resources of a small group of farmers and their families, and must have involved collaboration between perhaps 20 or 30 small local groups. This in turn implies a central organization, as well as a

certain community of interest between the local groups, and suggests that areas were already ruled by a chief or a council of elders, or very likely both.

What were the camps for? They may have been places at which local people gathered for public meetings, the settlement of disputes and the judgement of crimes, and for markets, feasts and festivals. It looks as if they were also centres for religious and magical ceremonies. At some of them – including Hambledon Hill and Windmill Hill – human skulls were found in the ditches, along with stone axes, pottery and cattle bones. Were these offerings to the gods? Or perhaps they were connected with rites for the dead, for another possibility is that the camps were sites where the bodies of the honoured dead were exposed on wooden platforms to rot before their bones were buried under long barrows.

Traces of the concentric ditches of a Neolithic causewayed camp, the first one recognized in Britain, can be seen on Knap Hill, near Alton Barnes in Wiltshire.

Camp SZ 483842 is a promontory fort above Gatcombe, with an irregular rampart standing up to 10 ft (3 m) high. It was probably the tribal centre of the island in the last centuries BC. The **Long Stone** SZ 408843, ½ mile (804 m) N of Mottistone, is a 13-ft (4.2-m) standing stone, one of a pair. The other lies beside it. They are close to the E end of a long barrow of about 3500 BC. **Michael Moorey's Hump** SZ 536874, ½ mile N of Arreton, is a round barrow over 6 ft (1.8 m) high. It takes its name from a man who was hanged on a gibbet there in 1730.

Knap Hill, Wiltshire

SU 121636, 1 mile (1.6 km) NE of Alton Barnes. Traces of a causewayed camp of about 3500 BC can be seen on this steep hill above the Vale of Pewsey. Across the road, on Walker's Hill to the W, is **Adam's Grave** SU 112634, a conspicuous long barrow of the same period, 200 ft (61 m) long and 20 ft (6 m) high. Traces of the stone burial chamber are visible at the E end.

Knowlton Rings, Dorset

SU 024100, *Dept of the Environment*. This site is a remarkable example of the Christian Church taking over a pagan sacred site. A ruined church stands inside the bank of a Neolithic henge. The henge, with a diameter of 320 ft (97 m), is the central circle of 3 in a line running

An aerial view of part of the mysterious Dorset Cursus, whose parallel banks run across country for almost 6 miles (9.6 km). It may have been used for funeral processions.

A ruined medieval church stands inside a Neolithic henge at Knowlton Rings in Dorset, an example of Christianity taking over an old pagan sacred site.

NW/SE. Not much is visible of the other 2. The S one is cut by the B3078 road. To the E of the central circle is an enormous round barrow, 20 ft (6 m) high and 125 ft (38 m) across, covered with trees. There are other round barrows nearby.

Not far to the N is the **Dorset Cursus** ST 970123 to SU 040191, which is the largest of its kind. A pair of banks about 100 yards (90 m) apart, with ditches outside them, run over hill and dale for about 6 miles (9.6 km), parallel to and S of the A354 Blandford–Salisbury road. Much of the cursus is no longer visible, but the SW end is 1 mile (1.6 km) NW of Gussage St Michael, near 2 long barrows on Thickthorn Down. It then runs NE up Gussage Hill round another long barrow, and can also be seen from B3081 on Bottlebush Down. There are more long barrows further on, and numerous round barrows were afterwards sited near the cursus, testifying to its sacredness. Constructing the cursus took $1\frac{1}{4}$ million man hours of work and required the shifting of over 6 million cubic feet (170,000 cubic metres) of chalk, so it was clearly important to those who built it. What it was for, however, is a mystery. It may have been used for funeral games, races or processions

Maiden Castle from the air. Complicated entrances were constructed at the E and W ends of this great fort to slow attackers down and expose them to a hail of slingshot.

connected with the cult of the dead who were buried in the long barrows. An alternative, or additional, possibility is that the cursus and the barrows provided sightlines to risings and settings of the sun and the moon in about 2500 BC, including a line to the setting sun at midwinter.

At **Oakley Down** SU 018173, N of B3081 and E of A354, is a notable cluster of Bronze Age round barrows of various types. Cutting across 2 of them at the E side is the impressive line of Ackling Dyke, the Roman road from Dorchester to Old Sarum, which also crosses the Dorset Cursus.

Maiden Castle, Dorset

SY 670885, *Dept of the Environment*, off A354, SW of Dorchester. One of the showpieces of England, this huge and thrilling hillfort, lying like a great beached whale, covers an area of about 47 acres (19 ha). It was excavated in the 1930s by Sir Mortimer Wheeler. The defences visible today date mainly from the first century BC. There are elaborate entrances at the W and E ends, with towering ramparts, designed to make the approach as slow and difficult for attackers as possible. At the gates slingers took station, with caches of pebbles collected from Chesil Bank

This view of the Maiden Castle ramparts gives an idea of the size and strength of the defences, which make it one of the most impressive strongholds in the country.

to fire at the enemy. In AD 44, however, the Second Legion Augusta, commanded by Vespasian, a future Roman emperor, successfully stormed the E gate. The skeletons of 38 of the defenders were found in a mass grave there. Each had been lovingly supplied with a joint of meat and a flagon of beer for the next world. One had a Roman catapult bolt embedded in his spine. After a time the fort was abandoned, but in the fourth century AD a temple was built on the E end of the hill, where its foundations can still be seen.

Long before, in about 3500 BC, a causewayed camp had been constructed on the E hilltop, though there is nothing of it to be seen now. Later an enormous barrow, 1800 ft (546 m) long, was built on the hill. The bodies of 2 children were found buried under its E end, perhaps as a foundation sacrifice. Also discovered was the body of a young man who had been mutilated and whose brain had been removed – suggesting possible ritual cannibalism – though the date of his death is uncertain.

In about 350 BC the hilltop was fortified. The defences were strengthened and enlarged a hundred years later, and a woman was buried at the point where the new rampart met the old, as a foundation sacrifice to 'reinforce' the join with her life energy. A small town of stone and wooden huts flourished on the hill, and the fortifications were rebuilt twice more, until the ramparts towered up 50 ft (15 m) above the ditches.

Marden, Wiltshire

SU 091584. The road from Marden to Beechingstoke crosses part of a large oval henge, built in about 2000 BC, with a bank and internal ditch. The River Avon formed the boundary on the S and W. A circular timber building, 30 ft (9 m) in diameter – perhaps a priests' college – stood inside the henge, as at Durrington Walls, near Stonehenge.

The elliptical ring of the Nine Stones near Winterbourne Abbas, concealed in a grove of trees by the roadside.

Maumbury Rings, Dorset

SY 690899. The Roman amphitheatre on this site outside Dorchester was built on what had long before been a Neolithic henge. In the ditch were found pits, up to 35 ft (10.5 m) deep, filled with fragments of human skulls, tools, broken pottery, the skulls of stags with the antlers attached, the jawbones of pigs and fertility carvings. The place had a long history as a ceremonial centre. In 1706 a woman named Mary Channing was executed by strangling on the floor of the amphitheatre for poisoning her husband.

The Nine Stones, Dorset

SY 611904, *Dept of the Environment*, beside A35, 5 miles (8 km) W of Dorchester, near Winterbourne Abbas. Thundering traffic can make stopping a little difficult. The circle is concealed in a copse and is unusual in being in a valley. There are 9 stones in an ellipse about 25 ft (7.5 m) across, the largest weighing about 8 tons. About ½ mile (804 m) to the W, on both sides of A35, is **Poor Lot** SY 588907, a fine agglomeration of various types of round barrow, with 2 long barrows to the SW.

Old Sarum, Wiltshire

SU 138327, *Dept of the Environment*, 2 miles (3.2 km) N of Salisbury on A345, best viewed from the W on A360. Mainly of interest now for its Norman castle and the foundations of a cathedral, but a hillfort crowned this height in prehistoric times, commanding a ford over the River Avon. The massive Iron Age ramparts were rebuilt by the Normans. Five Roman roads met here.

Old Winchester Hill, Hampshire

SU 641206, 2 miles (3.2 km) S of West Meon. Commanding hillfort with fine views, in a national nature reserve. There are bowl barrows to be found both inside and outside the fort.

Pilsdon Pen, Dorset

ST 413013, 2 miles (3.2 km) SW of Broadwindsor, reached from the N side of B3164. The highest hill in Dorset, just over 900 ft (274 m), it has wonderful views and a hillfort with double banks and ditches. A low mound of earth inside shows where a large wooden building once stood round an open courtyard. It may have been a temple. The mounds in the SE area were used in modern times for breeding rabbits.

Pimperne, Dorset

ST 917104, 3 miles (4.8 km) NE of Blandford Forum. Conspicuous Neolithic long barrow, on N side of A354, 9 ft (2.7 m) high and 330 ft (100 m) long.

An aerial view of Old Sarum, showing the remains of the Norman castle and cathedral. The hilltop was fortified much earlier, before the Roman conquest.

Part of the defences of the fort on Pilsdon Pen, perched on the highest hill in Dorset, with splendid views.

The Ridgeway Path

Opened in 1973 for walkers and cyclists, this path follows the line of a prehistoric track from near Avebury across the chalk uplands to the Thames at Streatley, near Goring. There it joins another ancient route, the **Icknield Way**, to run as far as Ivinghoe Beacon in Buckinghamshire. The track was part of the important prehistoric route between Wessex and Norfolk, and passes close to many interesting sites, including Barbury Castle, Liddington Castle, Wayland's Smithy and the Uffington White Horse.

St Catherine's Hill, Hampshire

SU 484276, 1 mile (1.6 km) s of Winchester on the E of A33. Inside this hillfort of about 400 BC are the ruined medieval chapel of St Catherine and a maze which, according to tradition, was built by the boys of Winchester School.

Stonehenge, Wiltshire

SU 123422, *Dept of the Environment*, beside A344, 2 miles (3.2 km) w of Amesbury. The greatest temple of its kind in Europe, and the most famous prehistoric monument in all Britain, can look disappointingly small and unromantic at first sight. It is so crowded, with half a million visitors a year, that on most days no one is allowed close to the stones and it helps to take binoculars.

The Stonehenge to be seen today has been standing there in much its present form for 3500 years, and is the culmination of three main phases of building and alteration going back 1300 years beyond that. The sacred area is bounded by a circular earth bank, originally 20 ft (6 m) wide and 6 ft (1.8 m) high, with a ditch outside it. The entrance is through a gap to the NE, pointing towards sunrise at midsummer over a 35-ton pillar called the Heel Stone (now leaning at an angle), 100 ft (30 m) away from the circle. This henge was the first temple constructed here, in about 2800 BC, and is known as Stonehenge I.

For years Stonehenge I must have been overshadowed by the far grander complex at Avebury, but in about 2100 BC Stonehenge II was built: 80 bluestones weighing 4 tons or so each were laboriously brought to the site from

The towering sarsen pillars at Stonehenge, locally called Saracens (hence 'sarsen'), were brought from 20 miles (32 km) away to the N and erected in a horseshoe surrounded by a circle.

At dawn on Midsummer Day an observer at the centre of Stonehenge, looking out through one of the great trilithons, sees the sun rise dramatically above the 35-ton Heel Stone.

A great variety of round barrows are grouped together at the Winterbourne Stoke crossroads, near Stonehenge. Most of them seem to be aligned on the older Neolithic long barrow near the roundabout.

another sanctuary over 100 miles away – the Prescelly Mountains in the SW corner of Wales. They were erected inside the henge in a double circle. An avenue running between banks and ditches was built from the henge's entrance towards the River Avon, 2 miles away, perhaps marking the last stage of the bluestones' journey.

Not long after this, the bluestone circles were removed and massive sarsen stones, weighing 25 to 50 tons each, were hauled to the site from the downs 20 miles (32 km) away to the N (Stonehenge IIIa). They were erected in a ring of 30 uprights joined across the top by lintels. Inside this circle 10 even larger uprights, also capped by lintels, were arranged in the shape of a horseshoe.

Later still, further alterations were made (Stonehenge IIIb) and a 16-ft (4.8-m) bluestone, now called the Altar Stone, was set upright at the centre of the complex. Finally, in about 1550 BC, the monument reached its present form when a horseshoe of bluestones was set up inside the sarsen horseshoe, and a circle of bluestones was placed between the sarsen horseshoe and the sarsen circle (Stonehenge IIIc).

Stonehenge was a temple and an expression of the power and grandeur of the ruling class which created it. It was also closely related to astronomy, the calendar and its creators' concepts of the order of the universe, which it no doubt embodied in stone. The whole monument is aligned to the midsummer sunrise and it seems that from the beginning it was used for observing risings and settings of the sun and moon. It is so sited that the extreme northern and southern risings and settings are at right angles to each other. A few miles north or south this would not be the case, which suggests that Stonehenge was deliberately sited where it is on the basis of accurate astronomical knowledge and a high regard for order, precision and symmetry. Hence the need to drag the huge stones to the site rather than build the temple 20 miles further north.

Stonehenge was still in use in 1100 BC, giving it a life of at least 17 centuries. The number of barrows close to it – the tombs of chieftains and aristocrats – suggests that it was the Westminster Abbey of its day, a place of worship for pilgrims from all over England, and even from abroad, to which the great were taken for burial.

One of the largest concentrations of barrows, with an example of almost every type, is on **Normanton Down** SU 118413 (*National Trust*), ½ mile (804 m) to the s. Burials of warrior chiefs were found here, equipped with bronze daggers and ornaments of gold and amber. There is another concentration where the A303 and A360 cross at **Winterbourne Stoke** SU 101417, (partly *National Trust*), including a well-preserved Neolithic long barrow, visible from A303 to the E of the roundabout. Just to the N of Stonehenge is the **Cursus** SU 124430, which is not open to the public. It runs for 1¾ miles (2.8 km) between banks and ditches, and may have been used for funeral games, races or processions.

About 2 miles NE of Stonehenge is **Woodhenge** SU 151434 (*Dept of the Environment*), on A345 1 mile (1.6 km) N of Amesbury. Little is left there now, but markers indicate the position of posts which appear to have supported a large circular wooden building, possibly with an open courtyard in the middle. Near the centre a cairn of flints marks the grave of a 3-year-old child, apparently a human sacrifice, killed by a blow on the head. The building was orientated to the midsummer sunrise and surrounded by a ditch and bank built in about 2300 BC.

Close by to the N is **Durrington Walls** SU 150437, where there is even less to be seen now, but in about 2550 BC an extremely large henge was constructed here, with a ditch up to 18 ft (5.4 m) deep and a bank 10 ft (3 m) high, gleaming white originally, enclosing an area of about 30 acres (12 ha). Inside stood a number of large wooden roundhouses. It may be that these and Woodhenge, built later, were the palace and court of a dynasty of kings, or priest-kings, who organized the building of Stonehenge nearby. Perhaps they were also the prehistoric equivalent of a monastery, where priests lived, pursued their studies in astronomy and mathematics, and trained their successors.

Interesting finds and displays related to the Stonehenge area and other Wiltshire sites can be seen at the Devizes and Salisbury museums.

Yarnbury Castle, Wiltshire

SU 035404, N of A303, 2 miles (3.2 km) W of Winterbourne Stoke. This hillfort with massive earthworks and an elaborate entrance at the E end was built in about 50 BC. Inside are traces of an older, smaller stronghold. A famous annual sheep fair was held here for centuries until 1916, and is mentioned in Hardy's *Return of the Native*.

HOW WAS STONEHENGE BUILT?

The great sarsen pillars of Stonehenge stand up to 30 ft (9 m) high and weigh up to 50 tons apiece. On top of them massive stone lintels were hoisted up and held in place by mortise-and-tenon joints. Each of these lintels weighs as much as 7 or 8 family saloon cars.

That people without modern machinery should have been able to build a construction of this kind challenges the conventional popular view of prehistoric man as an inferior savage – brawny but brainless. Modern experiments have shown that the simple tools available in prehistoric times – picks and shovels, axes and hammers, timbers and leather or cowhair ropes – were far more efficient than is generally realized. They have also brought the fact home that the building of Stonehenge involved a remarkable feat of organization and administration, requiring the recruitment, housing, feeding and supply over many years of a labour force of hundreds or even thousands and the transportation of materials over daunting distances. This implies the existence of a strong central authority – possibly a king – able to command the necessary obedience and effort.

The bluestones, the smaller monoliths at Stonehenge, came from modern Dyfed and were probably

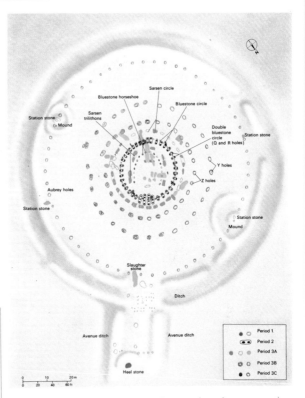

The massive lintels on the trilithons are curved and inclined, to allow for foreshortening when seen from the ground. They are held in place with mortice-and-tenon joints.

Plan of Stonehenge showing the complex of sarsens and bluestones arranged in horseshoes and circles. Near the outer edge is a ring of 56 pits, the Aubrey Holes, with a bank and ditch outside.

shipped on rafts along the coast of South Wales and up the Bristol Channel to where Avonmouth is now. They were transferred to boats and poled up the Avon and the Frome, and then perhaps dragged overland on sledges to the Wylye and the Salisbury Avon, which would bring them almost to Stonehenge after a journey of about 240 miles (384 km).

The sarsens, or blocks of sandstone, were brought about 20 miles (32 km) overland from near Avebury. Each block may have been tied on to a heavy sledge, which was pulled over rollers by teams of men heaving on ropes. At Stonehenge each stone was smoothed and shaped by pounding it with stone hammers. A hole was dug to receive it and it was manoeuvred into place and slowly raised upright with levers, timber ramps and ropes. Then the mortise-and-tenon joints were carved and the lintels gradually raised on ramps and levered into position.

Erecting the Stonehenge trilithons: a pit was dug for each sarsen pillar, which was raised on a ramp, levered into the hole and pulled upright, and then wedged in position with small stones. The lintels were raised on layers of staging and slid over on to the sarsens.

A tranquil section of the Pilgrims' Way, used by medieval pilgrims to Canterbury but dating from long before the Middle Ages : it was a prehistoric route between the Channel coast and Salisbury Plain.

LONDON AND THE SOUTH-EAST
GREATER LONDON, SURREY, WEST SUSSEX, EAST SUSSEX, KENT

THE growth of the capital has obliterated almost all traces of prehistoric man in the London area, but the city's museums have a great wealth of finds from south-east England and further afield. The Thames valley was a major route from and to the rest of Europe in almost unimaginably distant times, long before Britain became an island, when the Thames itself was still a tributary of the Rhine. In the Old Stone Age bands of hunters travelled along it, following the game herds on which they preyed, and the oldest human remains in Britain were discovered close to the Thames, at Swanscombe in Kent.

By land there was an old route, now called the Pilgrims' Way, from Kent to Wessex along the southern slopes of the North Downs. There are a few hillforts on the North Downs in Surrey and Kent, and an interesting group of Neolithic stone tombs in Kent, on either side of the Medway, near Maidstone, notably Kit's Coty House and Coldrum.

To the south was the vast forest of the Weald. Groups of Middle Stone Age hunters penetrated into the Weald and began to clear patches of the woodland by burning. They were succeeded by Neolithic farmers, and the Weald later became one of England's principal sources of iron. The largest surviving area of the Weald forest with any claim to antiquity is Ashdown Forest, near Wych Cross to the south of East Grinstead, with another patch in St Leonard's Forest, near Horsham.

The South Downs were probably lightly wooded in prehistoric times – not bare and grassy as they are now. They were cleared by generations of New Stone Age farmers, with fire and stone axes, who also settled on the Channel coast to the south and in the river valleys which cut through the Downs. Along the hilltops ran a prehistoric track, which is now the South Downs Way footpath and bridlepath. It runs past camps, barrows and hillforts in lovely walking and riding country, with wonderful views.

Museums of interest
Brighton Museum & Art Gallery; Museum of Canterbury; Guildford Museum; Barbican House Museum, Lewes; British Museum, London; British Museum (Natural History), London; Museum of London; Maidstone Museum & Art Gallery; Weald & Downland Open Air Museum, Singleton; Worthing Museum & Art Gallery.

Made early in the first century AD, perhaps for presentation to a temple, the Battersea Shield is over 2 ft 9 in (84.5 cm) long. The glass studs in the central roundel look like owlish faces.

Like the Battersea Shield, the Waterloo Helmet was recovered from the Thames and is now in the British Museum. It was made in the first century BC, of bronze, possibly for a god's statue.

PLACES TO VISIT

Chanctonbury Ring is a well-known Sussex landmark. The clump of beeches was planted inside the ramparts of an Iron Age hillfort.

Abinger Common, Surrey

TQ 112459. Mesolithic pit shelter, with small private museum, near Abinger Manor: key from owners. A V-shaped pit was dug here, about 14 ft by 10 ft (4.2 m by 3 m) and 3 ft (1 m) deep, and used as a sleeping place by Middle Stone Age hunters. It was probably roofed over with branches or skins supported on posts.

Bigbury Camp, Kent

TR 116576, on the Pilgrims' Way, w of Canterbury, 1 mile (1.6 km) NE of Chartham Hatch. The hillfort here was stormed by Julius Caesar's Seventh Legion in 54 BC, but has been far more severely damaged by farming, quarrying and building than it was by the Romans. Found here was an iron slave-gang chain, 18 ft (5.4 m) long, with collars for the slaves, a relic of the flourishing trade in exporting slaves from Britain to the Continent before the Roman conquest.

Caesar's Camp, Greater London

TQ 224711. Fort of the third century BC on the golf course on Wimbledon Common. The rampart was originally 30 ft (9 m) thick, revetted with timber, and the ditch was 12 ft (3.6 m) deep. Caesar's troops may have paused here before crossing the Thames.

Chanctonbury Ring, West Sussex

TQ 139121, on the South Downs Way, near Washington. The clump of beeches, a famous landmark, was planted in the eighteenth century inside the ramparts of an Iron Age fort. The remains of a small Romano-British temple were found in the centre. More defences lie to w and SE.

Chichester Dykes, West Sussex

These earthworks are about 2 miles (3.2 km) N of Chichester, with one stretch running from West Stoke across the River Lavant to Boxgrove Common. They were probably constructed in the first century BC to protect the capital of the Atrebates, the Celtic tribe in this area. The capital may have been where Chichester is now, or near Selsey, or it may have been engulfed by the sea.

Cissbury Ring, West Sussex

TQ 139080, *National Trust*, near Findon, 2 miles (3.2 km) N of Worthing. This large and impressive South Downs hillfort commands fine views. In about 350 BC a rampart of chalk was constructed, 30 ft (9 m) thick at the base, 15 ft (4.5 m) high, containing 60,000 tons of chalk and faced with no fewer than 10,000 upright timbers. The entrances were at the S and E. The boundary banks of fields of the Roman period can be seen in and outside the fort. Inside the W end of the fort and outside the S entrance are the hummocks and dips of one of the largest prehistoric flint mines in England. Mining began here in about 3500 BC, and over 200 shafts were dug with antler picks to depths of more than 40 ft (12 m), with galleries radiating below. At the foot of one shaft, 16 ft (4.8 m) down, was found the body of a young man, surrounded by a ring of carefully

At Coldrum are the massive sarsen stones of a Neolithic tomb, the burial vault of an important local family. The other stones once formed a kerb round a long mound that covered the tomb.

arranged blocks of chalk – perhaps a human sacrifice. In another shaft was the skeleton of a young woman, who seems to have fallen to her death accidentally.

Coldrum, Kent

TQ 654607, *National Trust*, 1 mile (1.6 km) NE of Trottiscliffe (locally pronounced 'Trosley'). In 1910 the skeletons of 22 men, women and children were found in this Neolithic tomb, probably several generations of the same family. Their bones showed that they suffered from rheumatism. With them were found the bones of ox, cat, deer, rabbit and fox – possibly offerings or the remains of feasts. The shining white mound which originally covered the tomb has long since vanished and the hulking stones of the burial chamber can be seen, with others strewn around. In a glass case in Trottiscliffe church are some of the bones from the tomb, with a human skull from elsewhere. The remains of another, partly restored, Neolithic tomb, **The Chestnuts** TQ 652592, are not far away, at Addington.

The Devil's Dyke, West Sussex

TQ 259111, near Poynings, reached from Brighton by a minor road off A2038. This celebrated and much-visited beauty spot, with tremendous views, has a promontory fort on the hill, protected by a single rampart and ditch. Below is the Dyke itself, a deep natural valley supposed to have been dug by the Devil in a single night. There was a late Iron Age village outside the fort to the SW.

Kit's Coty House is one of the most accessible of the Medway group of Neolithic tombs. Three uprights in the shape of a letter H support the giant slab of the capstone.

THE FIRST FARMERS

The earliest farmers in Britain came across the Channel from the Continent in about 4500 BC or earlier. They travelled in large coracles made of ox hide stretched over a wooden frame. With them they brought their seed-corn, a few cattle, sheep and pigs, and their dogs – of a breed similar to a modern fox terrier. They still fed themselves and their families partly by hunting, and the dogs gnawed the bones.

The farmers lived in small wooden huts, plastered with mud, roofed with grass or reeds and with the earth scooped out beneath so that the floor was below ground level. They made pottery and wore garments of cloth. They cleared woodland and scrub by cutting, ring-barking and burning, and planted seed in the ashes. When a couple of harvests had exhausted one patch they would clear another. Their essential tool was a stone axe, fixed to a wooden haft and used for felling trees, building houses and making sledges and boats. Grain was harvested with flint sickles and ground in stone querns. They also used wooden implements, deer antlers as picks and the shoulder blades of oxen as shovels.

Modern experiments have demonstrated that the stone axe is a far more effective tool than most people realize. One man working alone would have been able to clear close to half an acre (0.4 ha) of forest in a week. Gradually, as the farmers mingled with the earlier inhabitants and knowledge of farming spread, more land was cleared and a more settled system of agriculture developed, with farmsteads and hamlets of a few huts surrounded by a wooden palisade or an earth bank, close to small fields and cattle pounds. These were the precursors of village life as it has been known in England for countless generations. It was the people of these early peasant communities who built the mysterious causewayed camps and the massive long barrows, in which they reverently buried the elite of their dead.

Neolithic farmers used flint sickles to harvest grain, which they ground in stone querns.

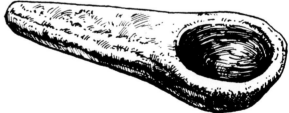

Pottery spoon: most of the implements familiar to us today had been invented by Neolithic times.

The Devil's Humps, King's Graves or Bow Hill Barrows, West Sussex

SU 807107. On Bow Hill, s of Stoughton, is a line of 4 large Bronze Age bell barrows, lying SE/NW, 10 to 12 ft (3 to 3.6 m) high and up to 130 ft (40 m) across. About 1 mile (1.6 km) to the SW is a twin bell barrow, with two mounds inside the same ditch. Nearby is **Goosehill Camp** SU 830127, an enclosure used for cattle from about 200 BC or earlier.

The Devil's Jumps, West Sussex

SU 825173, on the South Downs Way, 1 mile (1.6 km) s of Treyford. Five massive Bronze Age bell barrows stand in a line running NW/SE on Treyford Hill, with the remains of a sixth. One of them is 140 ft (43 m) in diameter and still stands 16 ft (4.8 m) high.

Firle Beacon, East Sussex

TQ 486058, 1 mile (1.6 km) SE of West Firle. The South Downs Way passes numerous round barrows here, and on top of Firle Beacon itself is a Neolithic long barrow orientated E/W, about 110 ft (33 m) long, 70 ft (21 m) wide and over 8 ft (2.4 m) high. According to local legend, it is the grave of a giant who was buried in a silver coffin. A car park and viewpoint are nearby.

Frensham Common, Surrey

SU 854407, *National Trust*. Near the Frensham Ponds are 4 Bronze Age bowl barrows in line.

Greenwich Park, Greater London

TQ 388771. In the W part of the park, to the W of the Observatory Building, are some small barrows. They were used again for burials in Saxon times.

Holmbury, Surrey

TQ 105430, 1 mile (1.6 km) SW of Holmbury St Mary. Double ramparts can be seen on the N and W sides of this Iron Age fort, which has fine views over the Weald. Two other hillforts not far away are **Anstiebury** TQ 153440, E of Leith Hill, and **Hascombe Hill** TQ 004386, near Hascombe.

Kit's Coty House, Kent

TQ 745608, *Dept of the Environment*, 1 mile (1.6 km) NW of Aylesford, to W of A229, on a hill with an attractive view. Fenced in with protective iron railings, this is one of the best-known Neolithic tombs in England. What can be seen is the burial chamber, formed by 3 huge upright stones, 8 ft (2.4 m) high, supporting a capstone which measures about 13 ft by 9 ft (3.9 m by 2.7 m). This dolmen was originally covered over by a huge mound, about 170 ft (52 m) long. A little way to the s is **Little Kit's Coty House** TQ 744604 (*Dept of the Environment*), a tumbled pile of stones in a clump of trees, the remains of a similar

The fort on the hill above the Devil's Dyke is protected by a ditch and bank about 200 yds (183 m) long and 12 ft (3.6 m) high, cutting off the promontory above the Dyke itself, a deep natural valley.

tomb which was knocked down by a farmer in 1690. Regarded with a certain awe within living memory, the stones were believed to help barren women to conceive, and it was said that you could never count them more than once and reach the same total. The word 'coty' is obscure. Could it be the same as the Cornish 'quoit'? Nearby, on the E side of A229, is the **Upper White Horse Stone** TQ 753603, 8 ft (2.4 m) long and 5 ft (1.5 m) high, vaguely resembling a horse. It may be all that is left of another tomb.

The Long Man of Wilmington, East Sussex

TQ 543095. This celebrated figure, restored in 1874, is cut into the chalk of the steep N face of Windover Hill, near Wilmington. Standing 230 ft (70 m) tall, with a pole (or spear?) in each hand, he is one of the largest representations of the human figure in the world. He was made to be seen from a distance to the N and is foreshortened if seen from close to. His date is extremely uncertain. The Long Man may be pre-Roman or Roman, or it has been suggested that he represents Woden, the great war-god of the Anglo-Saxons. He has also been identified as St Paul, or even Muhammad. Close to the figure are barrows, and hollows which may be the remains of flint mines. The South Downs Way bridleway runs nearby.

Mount Caburn or The Caburn, East Sussex

TQ 444089, N of A27, 2 miles (3.2 km) SE of Lewes. The

Cissbury Ring is an impressive South Downs hillfort, whose rampart was lined with 10,000 upright timbers. Flint was mined here many centuries earlier.

The Long Man of Wilmington, one of the world's largest depictions of the human figure, stands 230 ft (70 m) tall and was skilfully designed to be seen from a distance to the N.

massive outer rampart of this hillfort still stands 20 ft (6 m) above the bottom of the ditch and was originally faced with timber. It protected a settlement of about 300 people, living in huts of wattle and daub, and storing grain in pits deep in the chalk. Their chieftain may have ruled a sizeable area round about. The Romans took the fort and sacked it, however, and the settlement was abandoned. A castle was built on the hill in the Middle Ages.

Oldbury Hill, Kent

TQ 582562, *National Trust.* This steep hill to the w of Ightham, N of the A25, known as 'the Gibraltar of Kent', is crowned by a large fort covering 123 acres (50 ha), constructed in about 100 BC and later strengthened, presumably when word of the coming Roman invasion arrived. Caches of sling-stones were found inside the rampart. The entrances are at the S and NE, where a heavy timber gate was destroyed by fire. Below the fort, on the E slope of the hill, are two hollows in the rock (TQ 584565) which were used as shelters by Neanderthal hunters in about 35,000 BC. Many of the flint implements that they used were found on the site.

The Iron Age fort on Mount Caburn, near Lewes, was the stronghold of a chieftain who may

have dominated the country for miles around. It was stormed and sacked by the Romans.

Parliament Hill, Greater London
TQ 274865, on Hampstead Heath. To the NE of Hampstead Ponds, enclosed by railings, is a round barrow, about 10 ft (3 m) in height and now covered with bushes.

The Pilgrims' Way
Named for the medieval pilgrims who travelled to the shrine of St Thomas Becket in Canterbury, this was originally a prehistoric route from the Channel coast near Folkestone to Canterbury and along the North Downs to Guildford. The route continued on by a track now called the Harroway to Salisbury Plain. Some people trace it further still, to the tin mines in Cornwall, and it could conceivably have linked what is now the south-east of England to the rest of Europe before the Channel formed. Much of the original route is now covered by metalled roads, but there are stretches of track here and there on the Downs.

The Trundle, West Sussex
SU 877110, 4 miles (6.4 km) N of Chichester, on St Roche's Hill, overlooking Goodwood, with beautiful views. The name means 'the ring' or 'the hoop'. The hillfort was built in about 300 BC, enclosing a far older causewayed camp of about 3500 BC. The crouched skeleton of a woman buried under a heap of chalk blocks was found when the ditch of the causewayed camp was excavated.

Whitehawk, East Sussex
TQ 330048. In the Manor Hill Road area on Brighton racecourse faint traces can be seen of a Neolithic causewayed camp with 4 concentric ditches, in which human bones were found.

TRADE AND COMMUNICATIONS

A good deal of the present English road system may rest on prehistoric foundations. By the first century AD a network of routes covered much of the country and assisted the conquering Roman legions, who probably moved mainly along existing tracks. Some prehistoric roads were artificial constructions, like the wooden paths laid through the marshes of the Somerset Levels, but most of them came into existence naturally and gradually. Many of them may have started as routes followed by migrating reindeer and wild cattle.

Trade flourished in Neolithic times, and trade requires trade routes, along which, incidentally, news passes as well as goods. Boats plied along the coasts and rivers provided highways for traders in

The Sweet Track in the Somerset Levels, near Glastonbury. From as early as Neolithic times, artificial wooden roads were constructed through the tangles of the marshes.

The Somerset Levels tracks were constructed on the same principle as a modern railway track.

the interior, using dugout canoes and larger boats. A load of rough axeheads from the axe factories in Cumbria, for example, would have been carried far more easily by boat than packed on ponies or on human backs. Tools made of chert from the Isle of

Prehistoric traders used canoes made of hollowed out tree-trunks. Heavy loads were carried more easily by water than on land.

Portland in Dorset have been found as far away as Land's End in Cornwall, and in Gloucestershire, Surrey and Sussex. Some of this traffic would have gone by coastal boat, but some must have gone by land routes. The Pilgrims' Way along the North Downs may have been used by chert traders before 4500 BC.

Prehistoric tracks were not clearly defined like modern roads, but might sprawl out as much as half a mile (804 m) wide as travellers avoided ruts, potholes and puddles, and animals spread out to forage. In some cases there were alternative routes, a high one on the hills for summer and a lower, more sheltered one for winter travel.

Gold from Ireland and Wales was imported into England in the third millennium BC, and wandering Bronze Age smiths followed the tracks from one settlement to another to fill orders. A route is known to have crossed northern England from the Irish Sea at the mouth of the River Ribble, where Preston is today, by way of the Aire gap, the Wharfe valley, the Vale of York and the York Wolds to the east coast. Further south, the Icknield Way and the Berkshire Ridgeway connected Norfolk and Wessex. A route now called the Jurassic Way is thought to have run from the Bristol Channel and the Cotswolds to the Humber. There it would connect with a ferry, of the type discovered at Brigg, Humberside, in 1974. Dating from about 750 BC, it was made of thick oak planks, fastened together and caulked with clay and moss, making a platform 40 ft (12 m) long by 9 ft (2.7 m) wide, which could have carried heavy waggons. There were no doubt ferries of a similar sort on many other English rivers.

A central corridor runs through the Neolithic tomb at Stoney Littleton, with burial chambers opening off it. These massive stone tombs were family vaults and also shrines to powerful ancestors.

THE HEART OF ENGLAND
AVON, GLOUCESTERSHIRE, HEREFORD & WORCESTER, WEST MIDLANDS, WARWICKSHIRE, NORTHAMPTONSHIRE

PRIDE of place in this area must go to the Cotswold-Severn group of Neolithic chambered tombs, with their massive, whale-like long barrows. Belas Knap, Hetty Pegler's Tump and Stoney Littleton are good examples. The tombs are often in high positions with commanding views over the valleys below, perhaps to express the power and dominance of the families who built them, for they were both family monuments and shrines. The effort required to build them, in relation to the resources of the time, has been compared to the effort expended long afterwards in Egypt on the construction of the pyramids.

The barrows are generally wedge-shaped, about 100 to 175 ft (30 to 53 m) long and 50 ft (15 m) or so wide at the broader end. There are variations of layout, but usually the entrance was at the broad, eastern end and opened on to a gallery running longways under the mound, used for burials and with small crypts opening off it. Outside was a forecourt, used for rituals involving fires, feasting, dancing and possibly sacrifices. In some cases the entrance at the broad end of the barrow is a false one, which suggests that a formal portal at this end was required for symbolism or ritual, even when it had no practical use.

Also in this region, from rather later times, are the remains of a sacred complex of stone circles at Stanton Drew. From much later times there are splendid hillforts, including Croft Ambrey and Crickley Hill, which are both on National Trust property, and the great stronghold on the Herefordshire Beacon in the Malvern Hills. The fort on Bredon Hill must have been a grim sight in its heyday, with a row of human heads on poles above the gate. Another gruesome find was made there, the remains of 50 or more men hacked to bits and left in the entrance way. This seems to have been a legacy of warfare in pre-Roman times, though the Romans did destroy several hill strongholds here when they reduced the region to obedience, in about AD 48.

Museums of interest

Birmingham Museum & Art Gallery; City of Bristol Museum & Art Gallery; Cheltenham Art Gallery & Museum; City Museum & Art Gallery, Gloucester; Hereford City Museum & Art Gallery; Central Museum & Art Gallery, Northampton; Stroud Museum; Woodsprings Museum, Weston-super-Mare.

At the E end of Hetty Pegler's Tump an enormous stone lintel is supported on uprights framing a modern door. When the tomb was excavated 2 human skeletons were found in the forecourt.

PLACES TO VISIT

Arthur's Stone, Hereford and Worcester
SO 319431, *Dept of the Environment*, 1 mile (1.6 km) N of Dorstone, on Merbach Hill, above the head of the Golden Valley. The giant 25-ton capstone of this chambered tomb of about 3500 BC rests on 9 uprights. Most of the covering mound has gone. According to different legends, this was the burial place of King Arthur himself or of a king or a giant whom he killed.

Aveline's Hole, Avon
ST 476587, in Burrington Combe. The cave is on the E side of B3134, on the opposite side of the road from the 'Rock of Ages', the cleft rock in which Augustus Toplady sheltered from a storm in the 1760s and wrote the famous hymn. When discovered in 1797, the cave had 50 human skeletons in it, as well as flint tools, a barbed harpoon and a necklace of seashells. It had been inhabited by Stone Age hunters in about 12,000 BC.

Bagendon, Gloucestershire
SP 017600, W of A435, 2 miles (3.2 km) N of Cirencester. The earthworks here protected the tribal capital of the Dobunni, the Celtic people of the area, early in the first century AD. They covered about 200 acres (81 ha). Coins were minted here and pottery was imported from Italy.

Belas Knap, Gloucestershire
SP 021254, *Dept of the Environment*, 2 miles (3.2 km) S of Winchcombe, off minor road to Charlton Abbots: the name means 'beacon mound'. This restored megalithic tomb of about 3500 BC is one of the finest examples of its kind. The mound is 174 ft (52 m) long, 60 ft (18 m) wide at

According to one legend, King Arthur was buried under the huge 25-ton capstone of this Neolithic tomb, known as Arthur's Stone.

The burial vaults inside the Neolithic tomb of Belas Knap are reached by entrances in the side of the mound, which were originally sealed off.

the maximum, and 13 ft (3.9 m) high, orientated N/S and revetted by a drystone wall. The burial chambers inside are reached by short passages in the sides of the mound, which were originally sealed off. At the N end is a dummy entrance, blocked up, facing on to a forecourt between

At the N end of the Belas Knap long barrow is a false entrance facing on to a forecourt between two curving hornworks. The forecourt was used for rituals of the cult of the dead.

2 curving hornworks. Traces of fires were found in the forecourt and in the rubble blocking the false entrance were a man's skull and the bones of 5 children. The remains of more than 30 people were found inside the tomb itself. Curiously, some of them seem to have suffered a heavy blow to the head before or just after death.

Blaise Castle, Avon
ST 558784, in a public park at Henbury, on the N outskirts of Bristol. To the SW of Blaise Castle House Museum is a hillfort of the third century BC, with double ramparts. Nearby is another small fort, **King's Weston** ST 557782, where the remains of 10 or more bodies were found in 1966.

Borough Hill, Northamptonshire
SP 588626, 1 mile (1.6 km) E of Daventry. The BBC radio station which was built on the hill in 1925 cuts off much of the fort, but a formidable bank, ditch and outer bank can be seen on the golf course at the N end. The Royalist army camped on the hill before the battle of Naseby in 1645.

Bredon Hill, Hereford and Worcester

SO 958402, off B4080, NE of Tewkesbury. The whale-backed 960-ft (292-m) hill commands superb views of 'the coloured counties' below, as A.E. Housman wrote in his famous poem 'A Shropshire Lad'. On the N side is a strong promontory fort with 2 lines of ramparts and ditches. The outer defence line was constructed first, in about 300 BC, and the inner one about 150 years later. The entrance passage through the inner defences had a bridge over it, carrying a sentry walk, and a timber gateway at the inner end. Severed heads stuck on poles grinned down from above the gate, as trophies and probably also as

There are marvellous views from Bredon Hill to the Malvern Hills and across the Vale of Evesham to the Cotswolds and Shakespeare country. A formidable fort was constructed on the hill in Celtic times.

By the first century BC as many as 1500 people may have lived in the magnificent fort on the Herefordshire Beacon, in the Malvern Hills.

guardians of the fort. Early in the first century AD, before the Romans came, the stronghold was attacked by a war-party. The gate was burned down and the bodies of 50 men, cut to pieces, were left lying in the entrance. Presumably they were either killed defending the fort or were slaughtered out of hand after it had been taken. The eighteenth-century tower inside the defences is known as Parson's Folly. On a spur looking s towards the Cotswolds is **Conderton Camp** SO 972384. This was a fortified village in the first century BC.

Burrow Hill, Warwickshire
SP 304850, SE of Corley, looking over Coventry from the NW. This hillfort, dated between 50 BC and AD 50, has a bank over 6 ft (1.8 m) high in places.

Cadbury Camp, Avon
ST 454725, *National Trust*, on Tickenham Hill, N of B3130, 3 miles (4.8 km) E of Clevedon. Large hillfort with double ramparts, occupied in pre-Roman and Roman times.

Clifton Down Camp, Avon
ST 566733, in a public park near the Old Observatory, Clifton. Sections of the earthworks of a promontory fort can still be seen. On the opposite side of the spectacular Avon gorge, in the nature reserve of Leigh Woods, is **Stokeleigh Castle** ST 559733 (*National Trust*), a far more impressive fort of about 200 BC, with triple ramparts. The inner one is a huge limestone bank, in places towering 33 ft (10 m) above the bottom of the ditch.

Crickley Hill, Gloucestershire
SO 927161, *National Trust*, N of A417, 1 mile (1.6 m) N of Birdlip. This Cotswolds promontory fort, with splendid views over the Severn valley, is protected by steep slopes on the N and S, and on the E by a curving rampart 10 ft (3 m) high, with an entrance to the N which is protected by an outer hornwork and large bastions flanking the gateway. Inside was a village with rectangular buildings up to 60 ft (18 m) long set along a street. Later, a large round house was built, 50 ft (15 m) in diameter, perhaps as a chieftain's hall. The fort, first built about 700 BC, is on the site of a much older Neolithic causewayed camp.

Croft Ambrey, Hereford and Worcester
SO 444668, *National Trust*. A spectacular fort, said to command a view of 14 counties from almost 1000 ft up (304 m), tops a ridge N of Croft Castle, near Mortimer's Cross. In about 550 BC there was a village on the plateau at

the top of the hill with rows of rectangular wooden houses. About 150 years later the present massive inner rampart was built and protected by outer banks and ditches. Later an area to the S and E was walled off, probably for pasturing cattle. The mound here may have been the site of a shrine. The Romans seem to have destroyed the place in AD 48. Its population has been estimated at between 500 and 900 people.

Dolebury, Avon
ST 450590, 1 mile (1.6 m) SE of Churchill, off A38. An imposing Mendips hillfort in a dominating position with fine views. There are traces of lead mines inside, and earth workings which are the remains of rabbit warrens.

Haresfield Beacon, Gloucestershire
SO 825090, *National Trust*. A rampart encloses the top of

This view of the Herefordshire Beacon from the air shows the earthwork defences running along the contours of the narrow ridge. The mound in the centre is all that is left of a twelfth-century castle.

Ring Hill, with an outlying earthwork to the E, called the **Bulwarks**.

Herefordshire Beacon, Hereford and Worcester

SO 760400, in the Malvern Hills, SW of Little Malvern. This tremendous Iron Age fort with complex and formidable defences, and wonderful views, lies along a narrow 1100-ft (284-m) ridge, with earthworks following the contours. It was refortified again in the Middle Ages. At the centre is the twelfth-century castle mound, which stands inside the bank and ditch of a fort of the third century BC, covering 8 acres (3 ha), with entrances at the NE and SW. Later a much larger area was enclosed by massive additional earthworks, with 4 entrances, covering altogether 32 acres (13 ha). By this time, in the first century BC, there may have been as many as 1500 people living here. A prehistoric track runs up the hill to the W gate. Below the fort on the S side is Clutter's Cave or Hermit's Cave, which may have been occupied by a hermit in medieval times, and the nearby spring called Walm's Well is said to have healing properties.

Hetty Pegler's Tump or Uley Tumulus, Gloucestershire

SO 790000, *Dept of the Environment*, off B4066, 1 mile (1.6 km) N of Uley, on high ground above the Severn: key at nearby farm, torch needed. Another famous Neolithic tomb, with a mound 120 ft (37 m) long and 85 ft (26 m) wide, standing 10 ft (3 m) high, orientated E/W. It gets its name from the wife of one of its seventeenth-century owners. Inside were 5 burial chambers opening off a gallery 22 ft (6.6 m) long and 5 ft (1.5 m) high, containing 20 or more burials. In the forecourt outside the E entrance were found 2 human skeletons which had been buried with the jaws of boars. Whether these were sacrifices, offered to the dead when the tomb was finally sealed off, is not clear.

Inside Hetty Pegler's Tump a low passage, constructed of stone slabs and drystone walling, gave access to 5 burial chambers.

Uleybury hillfort on a steep spur near Hetty Pegler's Tump commands magnificent views. The main entrance was at the N corner.

Above Uley, on a steep spur with magnificent views, is **Uleybury** promontory fort, ST 784989. On the W side of B4066, about 1 mile N of Hetty Pegler's Tump, **Nympsfield Long Barrow** SO 794013 is in a public picnic area. This Neolithic chambered tomb has lost its roof and covering mound. Cross-shaped, with burial chambers off a central gallery, it is orientated E/W. The remains of 20 or more people were found inside. Some of the bones had been scorched by fire.

An interesting Neolithic tomb was discovered a little over 200 yards (182 m) to the N under a round barrow: **Soldier's Grave** SO 794015 was shaped like a boat, with a flat stern and a pointed prow, lying N/S, 11 ft (3.3 m) long and cut into the rock. Inside were the tumbled remains of 28 or more bodies with fragments of pottery and the bones of oxen, pigs and dogs. Were these the remains of funeral feasts or were the dead sent into the next world with joints of beef and pork for provisions and a faithful dog for company? The boat-shaped grave suggests a belief that the dead had to make a journey over water and recalls Celtic legends of magic islands across the sea in the west.

Hunsbury, Northamptonshire

SP 737584, on the S outskirts of Northampton, W of A43. Ironworking in the 1880s lowered the hillfort's interior by about 8 ft (2.4 m), making the ramparts, which are now tree-covered, look higher than they should. Many bronze and iron objects were found here, including parts of chariots and horse harness. The inhabitants in the first century BC had trade contacts as far away as Yorkshire and the south-west. One human skull discovered here had holes bored in it, perhaps so that it could be carried slung from a horse's neck.

King Arthur's Cave, Hereford and Worcester

SO 545155, in woods above the River Wye, 1 mile (1.6 km)

King Arthur's Cave, above the valley of the River Wye. Ashes from the campfires of Stone Age hunters were found on the ledge outside.

almost 8 ft (2.4 m) high, pierced with holes believed to be the result of weathering. Babies used to be pushed through the holes to prevent rickets. The stone may be all that is left of a Neolithic tomb. The fenced off Neolithic **Gatcombe Lodge** chambered tomb is close by to the N. To the S is the **Tinglestone Long Barrow** ST 882990, covered with trees, 130 ft (40 m) long and standing 6 ft (1.8 m) high, orientated N/S. On the N end of the barrow stands the **Tinglestone** itself, 6 ft (1.8 m) high. It is said that it runs across the field when midnight strikes on the clock of Avening church, 1 mile (1.6 km) to the S. Near the church are 3 stone burial chambers, ST 879983, moved here by the rector in 1806 from a neighbouring long barrow. The biggest chamber is about 6 ft (1.8 m) square, with a capstone covering 6 uprights and a 'porthole' cut into the uprights, through which a corpse could just have been manoeuvred.

Lydney Park, Gloucestershire
SO 616027, 1 mile (1.6 km) SW of Lydney. Known for its temple of the Celtic god Nodens, built in the fourth century AD inside a promontory fort of the first century BC. There were iron mines here in Roman times, and perhaps earlier.

Midsummer Hill, Hereford and Worcester
SO 761375, *National Trust*, in the Malvern Hills, 2 miles (3.2 km) SW of Little Malvern, N of A438. The fort here was occupied from about 450 BC until the Romans slighted it in AD 48. There were probably about 250 huts inside, rectangular and measuring about 11 ft (3.3 m) by 15 ft (4.5 m), neatly arranged in streets. Two hilltops are enclosed by the ramparts and there is a natural spring near the SW gate.

SW of Great Doward. Bones of animals including mammoth, woolly rhino and cave-bear were found in this cave, and Stone Age hunters camped here at intervals from about 12,000 BC. The ashes of their fires have been found on the ledge outside the cave, with animal bones and flint and bone implements.

The Long Stone, Gloucestershire
ST 884999, NE of Avening. A massive standing stone

THE HOUSES OF THE DEAD

The oldest impressive constructions in England are tombs, the long barrows built for the dead in Neolithic times, from before 4000 BC. The most striking thing about them is their size. They may be anything up to 300 ft (91 m) long and more than 50 ft (15 m) wide, with a bulk of thousands of tons, immensely larger than was needed merely to cover the tumbled bones inside. In chalk country newly made barrows would have shone blinding white, and they were often placed in commanding positions visible for considerable distances around. It was evidently important to the builders that these great tombs should be overwhelmingly impressive, massive and permanent and constructing them required authority and efficient organization.

The tombs were probably the family vaults of the ruling class, used for generations. They may contain the remains of 50 people or more, of both sexes, adults, children and newborn babies. They were not only tombs but also shrines where the living gathered to honour the powerful ancestors of the clan or tribal group and ask for their help and protection.

In southern and eastern England the barrows consist of earth or lumps of chalk, usually dug out of

*Artist's reconstruction of a wooden mortuary house, built like a ridged tent,
in which dead bodies were placed after being exposed to rot in
the open air.*

flanking ditches. Long before a barrow was built, however, corpses were laid out to rot on a platform, in a special area marked off by a ditch and often by a bank and a timber palisade. Later, the bones were put in a wooden mortuary house like a ridged tent, supported by huge posts, on the same site or some way away. In at least some cases the complete skin of an ox, with horns, head and hoofs, was hung over the mortuary house. Eventually, when enough bodies had accumulated, the barrow mound was heaped up over the mortuary house, which was sometimes burned down first, scorching the bones inside. The mound is usually wedge-shaped and stands higher at its wider end, above the bodies. This was normally to the east – the direction of sunrise and so, perhaps, of renewed life after the darkness of death.

In western England the huge mounds of earth or rubble were raised over 'chambered tombs' – burial chambers constructed of large boulders, which may have been stone equivalents of the wooden mortuary houses. The simplest variety are the dolmens, with a burial chamber formed by large upright stones and a capstone. Others are more complicated. The theory that the inspiration for these massive structures must have come from Egypt and the Near East, brought here by missionaries or colonists, has been abandoned with the discovery that many of them are much older than their supposed eastern antecedents.

What these tombs meant to those who built them we can only guess at. One theory is that they were artificial caves and symbolic wombs of the Earth Mother, from which the ancestors would one day be reborn. Almost certainly they were monuments of family and tribal pride, expressing the lasting identity of the group and a mixture of fear, affection and respect for the dead.

The stone circles at Stanton Drew formed part of a major sacred complex, comparable to Avebury in scale and of about the same date.

Minchinhampton Bulwarks, Gloucestershire

SO 858010, *National Trust*. On Minchinhampton Common, NW of the village, a mysterious, roughly bow-shaped earth bank and ditch, over a mile (1.6 km) long, curve from SW to NE. If this work was meant to protect Minchinhampton, the ditch seems to be on the wrong side, so it may have been built to defend the spur to the N. One possibility is that the British chieftain Caradoc (Caratacus) fortified the area during his resistance to the Romans after the fall of Colchester. The ditch was originally cut 6 ft (1.8 m) deep into rock and the bank was 16 ft (4.8 m) thick. There are more earthworks to the NW. Among the earthworks is a damaged barrow known as **Whitfield's Tump** SO 854017 because the Methodist missionary George Whitfield preached from its summit in 1743.

Notgrove, Gloucestershire

SP 096211, *Dept of the Environment*, S of B4068, 1 mile (1.6 km) NW of Notgrove. This Neolithic tomb, orientated E/W, had burial chambers opening off a long gallery. In the centre, sealed off, were the remains of a man in his fifties, inside a stone chamber with a domed roof. He was perhaps someone specially important or specially feared. Above his chamber were the bones of a girl in her late teens. Also found in the tomb were the remains of 6 or more adults, 3 children and a newborn baby, as well as animal bones. In the forecourt at the E end were discovered traces of fires, with animal bones and 2 human skeletons.

Rainsborough Camp, Northamptonshire

SP 526348, in beautiful country, 1 mile (1.6 km) NE of Aynho. The fort has an inner bank up to 15 ft (4.5 m) above the bottom of its ditch and an outer bank about 4 ft (1.2 m) high. The drystone walling to be seen dates from the eighteenth century, when the place was landscaped. Excavations in the 1960s showed that the fort's entrance on the W side was approached by a cobbled road which led through a passage 60 ft (18 m) long and 12 ft (3.6 m) wide to wooden gates flanked by C-shaped stone guard chambers and bridged by the rampart walk. The defences were built in the fifth century BC and after about a hundred years the fort was attacked and the gate was burned. The remains of a man in his thirties were found in the guard chamber to the S, with a hole in his skull, apparently from the blow that killed him. In the second century BC the stronghold was rebuilt and then abandoned again, and then reoccupied in Roman times.

Sodbury Camp, Avon

ST 761826. Fine hillfort on the Cotswolds' edge above Little Sodbury, W of A46. The main entrance was on the E, where the stone rampart is reddened, showing that the gateway was burned at some time.

Stanton Drew, Avon

ST 601634, partly *Dept of the Environment*. E of the village, off B3130, are the remains of what was once an impressive sacred complex of about 2600 BC, with 3 circles, traditionally known as **The Weddings** because the stones were said to be the members of a wedding party turned to stone for dancing and revelling on a Sunday. The central circle is the second largest in Britain (after Avebury), about 368 ft (112 m) in diameter, with 27 stones still visible, most of them fallen. A stone avenue leads E towards the River Chew and meets another avenue leading from the N circle. The third circle is to the SW, among trees. Aligned with the N and central circles is a cove or U-shaped arrangement of 2 huge uprights and a fallen stone, of unknown significance. It stands beside the churchyard, near the Druids Arms Inn. A line from the SW and central circles leads to **Hauteville's Quoit** ST 602638, a 7-ft (2.1-m) standing stone, now fallen, on the other side of the river.

Stoney Littleton, Avon

ST 735573, *Dept of the Environment*, about 1 mile (1.6 km) SW of Wellow, E of Peasedown St John. A torch is needed

A fossil ammonite was built into one of the jambs at the Stoney Littleton tomb entrance. Spiral patterns suggest the ebb and flow of life, waxing and waning, growth and decay, and perhaps the fossil was a symbol of life continuing after death.

The Stoney Littleton long barrow was restored in 1858, when it was described as 'the most perfect specimen of Celtic antiquity still existing in Great Britain'. In fact it goes back far beyond the Celtic period and was built about 5000 years ago.

to explore this tomb of about 3000 BC, which was restored in 1858. The mound is over 100 ft (30 m) long and stands 10 ft (3 m) high, orientated SE/NW. There is a horned forecourt with a low entrance, which has the cast of a fossil ammonite on one jamb. Was the spiral pattern of the shell related to the hope of a life after death (spirals are often symbols of the underlying patterns of life)? Inside is a walled and vaulted passage 48 ft (14.6 m) long and 4 ft (1.2 m) high, with 7 burial chambers off it. Numerous human bones were found inside in the nineteenth century.

Wappenbury, Warwickshire

SP 377693. The village is surrounded by the earthwork defences of a low-lying fort of the first century BC or early first century AD, close to and commanding 2 fords over the River Leam.

Windmill Tump, Gloucestershire

ST 932973, N of A433, 1 mile (1.6 km) SW of Rodmarton. Tree-covered and surrounded by a modern wall, this massive Neolithic barrow contained the remains of 13 or more people, including 3 children, aged 2, 3 and 12. Lying E/W, about 200 ft (61 m) long and 100 ft (30 m) wide, it has a dummy entrance at the E end with a forecourt in which were found animal bones and traces of fires.

Worlebury Camp, Avon

ST 315625, N of Weston-super-Mare. Overlooking the Bristol Channel, this fort is protected by ramparts up to 10 ft (3 m) high, flanked by ditches. On the E side pits can still be seen, dug 6 ft (1.8 m) down into the rock, used first for storing grain and later as rubbish pits. Skeletons were found in some of them and the fort seems to have been attacked at some time, by the Romans or perhaps by a war-band of hostile tribesmen.

The Ridgeway Path, near White Horse Hill. This prehistoric track, now an official path for walkers and cyclists, runs from near Avebury past many interesting sites to the Thames at Streatley, where it connects with the Icknield Way.

THAMES AND CHILTERNS
BERKSHIRE, OXFORDSHIRE, BUCKINGHAMSHIRE, BEDFORDSHIRE, HERTFORDSHIRE

THE Thames-Chilterns area was quite thickly populated when Julius Caesar's legions drove their way north into what is now Hertfordshire, but intensive farming and building have obliterated almost all traces of prehistoric farms and settlements, except from the air. Long before, in the Old and Middle Stone Ages, men had hunted in the Thames valley, the Chilterns and what were then the marshes of the Colne valley. In the New Stone Age important land and river routes crossed the area. Traders and travellers trod the Icknield Way along the edge of the Chilterns, to Wessex in one direction and to East Anglia in the other. The Thames was a highway connecting the interior of England with the sea and the Continent. The name Chilterns is apparently not English and not Celtic, which raises the intriguing possibility that it comes from a language spoken in England very long ago indeed, in remote pre-Celtic times.

The most famous and most fascinating prehistoric monument in this region, however, is Celtic.

The White Horse of Uffington attracts so many visitors that it is in danger of serious damage. The Celts loved horses for their swiftness and strength, their loyalty, their beauty and fierceness in battle, and several Celtic goddesses were closely associated with the horse. The White Horse is probably a representation of one of them, in horse form. Nearby is another famous site, Wayland's Smithy, a Neolithic tomb which is approaching 6000 years old, and on the Lambourn Downs not far away is one of the best assemblages of Bronze Age barrows in the country.

Further north, on a ridge along the Oxfordshire–Warwickshire border, stand the Rollright Stones, of sinister repute, the third major stone circle in England after Stonehenge and Avebury. The hillfort on top of Ivinghoe Beacon in Buckinghamshire is one of the first constructed in England, and at Wheathampstead in Hertfordshire are titanic earthworks which may be all that is left of the stronghold of Caswallon, the British war-leader who defied Julius Caesar.

Museums of interest
Buckinghamshire County Museum, Aylesbury; Luton Museum & Art Gallery; Ashmolean Museum of Art and Archaeology, Oxford; Pitt-Rivers Museum, Oxford; Reading Museum & Art Gallery; Verulamium Museum, St Albans.

Celtic coins showing horses, which the Celts loved and admired for their prowess in battle. The wheels are chariot wheels. The earliest coins minted in Britain are believed to date from about 100 BC.

These glass counters were found with the remains of a game board in a grave of the late first century BC at Welwyn Garden City. They were used in a game which may have resembled ludo.

PLACES TO VISIT

Alfred's Castle, Oxfordshire
SU 277822, on Swinley Down, 2 miles (3.2 km) SE of Ashbury; reached through Ashdown Park (*National Trust*), S of the Ridgeway Path. This small Iron Age hillfort has a bank up to 12 ft (3.6 m) above the bottom of the ditch. The bank was once faced with sarsen boulders, but they were taken away in the seventeenth century for the building of Ashdown House. The site is traditionally the place where King Alfred's army mustered in 871 before defeating the Danes at the battle of Ashdown.

Arbury Banks, Hertfordshire
TL 262387, 1 mile (1.6 km) SW of Ashwell. A farmstead stood on this low hill in the late centuries BC, protected by the rampart which can still be seen. Inside was a large circular house with outbuildings and grain storage pits. The Ashwell Village Museum illustrates life and work in the village from the Stone Age onwards (open on Sunday afternoons and at other times by appointment).

Boddington Camp, Buckinghamshire
SP 882080, 1 mile (1.6 km) E of Wendover. This tree-veiled Iron Age fort on a high ridge in magnificent Chilterns scenery has a rampart 13 ft (3.9 m) high in places, with a surrounding ditch.

Bulstrode Camp, Buckinghamshire
SU 994880. In the angle of the A40 and the A332 at Gerrards Cross is a large Iron Age fort covering 22 acres (9 ha), with double ramparts and ditches.

Caesar's Camp, Berkshire
SU 863657, 1 mile (1.6 km) S of Easthampstead, S of Ninemile Road. Part of this Iron Age fort is in a public recreation area. Its bank and ditch twist and turn to follow the 400-ft (121-m) contour line. A track runs S for 1 mile to the Devil's Highway, a Roman road from London to Silchester. It seems unlikely that Caesar was ever here.

Castle Hill or Sinodun Camp, Oxfordshire
SU 569925, 1 mile (1.6 km) SW of Dorchester on the Sinodun Hills. This fort above the River Thames commands wonderful views. It is protected by a deep ditch and an outer bank, and there may once have been an inner rampart as well. A Bronze Age barrow is visible to the SE. About 1 mile to the NE on the far side of the Thames is the **Dyke Hills** promontory fort, SU 574937. There was a village here in the late centuries BC, on the low ground between the Thames and the Thame, with 2 big banks and a ditch, the banks still 10 ft (3 m) high here and there. The Romans founded a small town between the Thames and the present village of Dorchester.

Cholesbury Camp, Buckinghamshire
SP 930073, 4 miles (6.4 km) E of Wendover. Cholesbury church is inside the perimeter of this tree-covered Chilterns fort, which may date from the second century BC.

Five Knolls, Bedfordshire
TL 006211, S of Dunstable on Dunstable Down, between B489 (which here follows the Icknield Way) and B4541. Despite the name, this is a group of 7 barrows dating from late Neolithic and Bronze Age times. One of them is a triple bell barrow, with three mounds enclosed by a single ditch. When the bowl barrow at the N end was excavated more than 90 skeletons were found close to the surface. About 30 of these had been buried with their hands fastened behind their backs, the victims of a mass execution in the fifth century AD. Others had been hanged some centuries later.

Grimsbury Castle, Berkshire
SU 512723, 4 miles (6.4 km) NE of Newbury, to SE of Hermitage. This fort was occupied in about 300 to 100 BC. Its ramparts follow the contour lines, with the original entrance in the W side, protected by an outlying earthwork, and others in the N and SE.

Grim's Ditch
Various Iron Age earthworks in this area share this name, though they may not all belong to the same system. They seem to have marked boundaries. One stretch is near the Ridgeway Path, to the E of A34. There is another section to the E of Wallingford and more stretches between Naphill, NE of West Wycombe, and Dunstable. A section can be seen near Redland End, SP 835023, in Buckinghamshire. This was possibly the boundary of the powerful Catuvellauni people, whose rulers included Caswallon and Cunobelin. More earthworks appear in the Charlbury-Woodstock area of Oxfordshire, with a section in Blenheim Great Park, SP 427183, crossed by the Roman road called Akeman Street. The bank was originally about 20 ft (6 m) thick and 6 ft (1.8 m) high, with a V-shaped ditch about 6 ft (1.8 m) deep and 20 ft (6 m) wide at the top.

Hoar Stone, Oxfordshire
SP 378236, 4 miles (6.4 km) SE of Chipping Norton, on the minor road from Lidstone to Fulwell. This megalithic tomb of about 3500 BC was originally covered by a mound. There are 3 upright stones, the tallest 9 ft (2.7 m) high, and 3 fallen stones left.

Inkpen or Combe Gibbet Long Barrow, Berkshire
SU 365623, on the downs SE of Inkpen. Dating from about

Cholesbury, the tree-clad defences of an Iron Age fort with double and triple ramparts.

Aerial view of the most accessible barrows on Lambourn Downs, which constitutes one of England's finest prehistoric cemeteries, containing bowl, bell, disc and saucer barrows and double bowl barrows.

3500 BC, this barrow is orientated E/W, with ditches on either side. It is about 150 ft (46 m) long and 50 ft (15 m) wide. On top of it is a reconstruction of the gibbet originally erected here in 1676. Not far off to the s is an enormous fort on **Walbury Hill** SU 374617, almost 1000 ft above sea level, with a rampart and ditch enclosing 82 acres (33 ha). There are entrances at the NE and SE, with outlying earthworks.

Ivinghoe Beacon, Buckinghamshire

SP 960169, *National Trust*, 1 mile (1.6 km) NE of Ivinghoe. A triangular hillfort of the late Bronze Age crowns the 760-ft (231-m) Beacon Hill, above the Icknield Way, with splendid views. It is one of the earliest forts in the country, and the rampart is said to be clumsily constructed owing to lack of experience. It was originally faced with horizontal timbers. The ditch was about 8 ft (2.4 m) wide and deep. There is a barrow on the summit of the hill and 2 more on the w side of the track leading from the car park to the fort.

Lambourn Seven Barrows, Berkshire

SU 328828, on Lambourn Downs – where strings of racehorses are exercised – 2 miles (3.2 km) N of Lambourn, straddling a minor road to Kington Lisle. This is one of the finest Bronze Age barrow cemeteries in England, with far more than 7 barrows in it, over 20 in fact. They were excavated in the 1850s, but not much is known about what was found. The accessible ones are in 2 rows running NW/SE on the NE side of the road. One is a double barrow, with twin mounds inside the same ditch. The skeletons of a dog and an ox were found in the N mound. To the NW of this barrow is a small saucer barrow. On the other side, to the SE, are a large bowl barrow, 100 ft (30 m) across and 10 ft (3 m) high, another bowl barrow, 70 ft (21 m) across and 7 ft (2.1 m) high, and a disc barrow about 100 ft (30 m) across. The second row is further from the road. Not much is left of the far older Neolithic long barrow to the NW, SU 323834, dating from about 4300 BC. The **Uffington White Horse** and **Wayland's Smithy** are not far away.

BODIES AND BARROWS

With the coming of the Beaker People and the Bronze Age, the old Neolithic long barrows went out of fashion and were replaced by round barrows. Still to be seen in their thousands, though thousands more have been destroyed, round barrows vary considerably in type and size. They occur singly or in groups, as at Lambourn, often arranged in straight lines. In chalk country they gleamed freshly white when they were new. Some had a standing stone on top or a carved or painted wooden post.

Barrow burial remained the prerogative of the elite, ordinary people presumably being shovelled below ground without much ceremony. The round barrows, though sometimes large, are generally not as massive and imposing as their Neolithic predecessors. One person would be interred at the centre of the barrow, sometimes accompanied by others, who may have been women and slaves killed to go to the afterworld with their master. Afterwards, as the years went by, other people – probably members of the same family – would be buried in the sides of the mound. Many barrows were designed from the outset to be used in this way.

The simplest and commonest type of round barrow is the bowl barrow – like an inverted pudding basin. Other types are the bell, disc, saucer and pond barrows (see diagram). The earth for the mound was usually dug out of a surrounding ditch. In the west and north, in stony territory, cairns of stones were used instead of earth mounds. Corpses were still exposed to rot before burial and some barrows were heaped over wooden mortuary houses.

As the Bronze Age wore on, cremation became increasingly the accepted custom. Sometimes a barrow was raised over the funeral pyre, but more often over an urn containing the cremated remains. Barrows gradually shrank in size and in the Iron Age were used less and less: in most cases, presumably, the body was cremated and the ashes scattered.

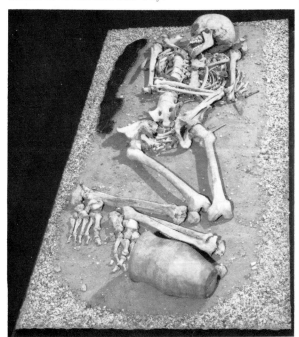

The Barnack Beaker burial: found with the body were a beaker, an archer's wristguard, a dagger and a bone pendant.

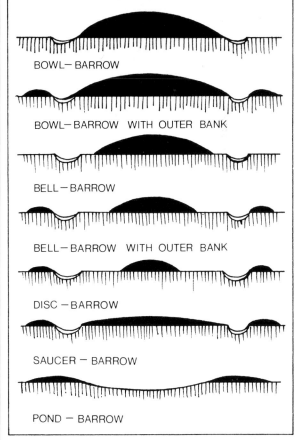

BOWL – BARROW

BOWL – BARROW WITH OUTER BANK

BELL – BARROW

BELL – BARROW WITH OUTER BANK

DISC – BARROW

SAUCER – BARROW

POND – BARROW

Members of powerful Bronze Age families were buried under round barrows of various types. Disc and saucer barrows were used more often for female than male burials.

The King Stone, like a great fang rotted away by time, is outside the Rollright circle on the edge of the hill. It may have been a marker for approaching travellers to the circle, and may also have been aligned on the star Capella.

Lyneham Barrow, Oxfordshire

SP 297211, in a field on the W side of A361, SW of Chipping Norton. The mound of a Neolithic tomb, damaged by ploughing, stands about 170 ft (52 m) long. It lies NE/SW and at the NE end is a solitary standing stone, 6 ft (1.8 m) high.

The Rollright Stones, Oxfordshire

SP 296308, 3 miles (4.8 km) NW of Chipping Norton, beside a minor road leading W off A34. On the S side of the road are the **King's Men**, more than 70 stones, stumps and fragments, anything from a few inches high to almost 7 ft (2.1 m) tall. These are the remains of perhaps 20 or so taller stones, which once stood in a perfect circle with a diameter of exactly 38 megalithic yards (104 ft/31.6 m). On the other side of the road, caged behind railings, is the **King Stone**, an outlying pillar about 8 ft (2.4 m) tall and 5 ft (1.5 m) wide, apparently aligned on the rising of the star Capella in 1790 BC. To the E of the circle are the stones called the **Whispering Knights**, which are the remains of a Neolithic tomb, with a capstone and 4 uprights, the largest of them more than 8 ft (2.4 m) high, enclosing a burial chamber about 6 ft (1.8 m) square.

Eaten away by time, the Rollright Stones have a sinister reputation and something of an eerie atmosphere. Legend says that they were a king and his men, turned to stone by a witch who then turned herself into an elder tree. They are said to be uncountable and there are rumours of them going down the hill by night to drink at a spring in the valley. Local people used to meet at the circle once a year for merrymaking and dancing, perhaps continuing a

The stones called the Whispering Knights are the remains of a Neolithic tomb, which stood here before the Rollright circle was erected.

The sun gleams on the Rollright Stones, originally a ring of about 20 tall stones in a perfect circle exactly 38 megalithic yards (31 m) in diameter.

tradition of fertility rites going back to the prehistoric period. Barren women used to press their breasts against the King Stone in hope of a child. There were reports of witches meeting here in Tudor times and again much more recently, during and since the 1940s.

Segsbury Camp or Letcombe Castle, Oxfordshire

SU 385845, on the Ridgeway Path E of Letcombe Basset. This fort of the second century BC has a single bank, formerly faced with massive sarsens. A human body was found buried in the S rampart, perhaps a foundation sacrifice to 'strengthen' the wall.

Therfield Heath, Hertfordshire

TL 342402, on a golf course S of A505, W of Royston. A long barrow of about 3000 BC, orientated E/W and about 8 ft (2.4 m) high, stands here with 8 Bronze Age round barrows up to 70 ft (21 m) across and 12 ft (3.6 m) high. In one of them 9 disarticulated skeletons were found. There are other barrows nearby.

The Rollright Stones range from fragments a few inches high to pillars almost 7ft (2.1 m) tall.

The site has a sinister reputation and is traditionally linked with witchcraft.

The surrealistic, superbly vigorous White Horse of Uffington may be a depiction of the Celtic goddess Epona, 'the great mare', protector of horsemen.

Uffington Castle and White Horse, Oxfordshire

SU 299864, *Dept of the Environment*, off B4507 and the Ridgeway Path, about 5 miles (8 km) W of Wantage. The 'castle' is the Iron Age fort on Whitehorse Hill, covering about 8 acres (3.2 ha), with 2 banks and ditches, and an entrance at the NW. Below the fort, cut into the turf on the steep hillside, is the famous White Horse, a strange, surrealistic and superbly vigorous beast which measures about 360 ft (109 m) from ear to tail and 130 ft (40 m) in height. It resembles horses on British coins of pre-Roman times and may have been cut in the first century BC as a representation of the Celtic deity Epona, 'the great mare', goddess of horses and protector of horsemen. The figure used to be scoured clean every 7 years by the local people in a festival that lasted for several days. It became connected with the legend of St George and a flat-topped hill below the Horse is called Dragon Hill and supposed to be the spot where the gallant saint killed the dragon. The horse cannot be seen properly from close by. There are good views of it from the N, from Great Coxwell church.

Near the Ridgeway, in a grove of trees, Wayland's Smithy is a Neolithic tomb built on top of an even older barrow. This view shows the whole of the entrance façade.

Tall sarsen columns frame the entrance to Wayland's Smithy where, according to legend, the White Horse's shoes were made. Gaps between the stones are filled in with drystone walling.

The Horse's shoes, according to legend, were made by Wayland the Smith, the lame smith of the gods in Anglo-Saxon mythology. **Wayland's Smithy** SU 281854 is a little over a mile off along the Ridgeway Path to the SW, in a grove of trees. Down into the eighteenth century it was said that if you left a horse beside the smithy with a penny in payment, he would be well shod by an unseen hand when you returned for him. The 'smithy' is in fact a megalithic tomb of the period 3700 to 3400 BC, built on top of an earlier barrow. The low mound is 180 ft (55 m) long by 48 ft (14.5 m) wide at its maximum, orientated SE/NW. At the southern end is a facade of 4 (originally 6) standing stones, 10 ft (3 m) high. Inside is a passage 20 ft (6 m) long, with burial chambers opening off it in a cross-shaped plan. The older tomb underneath cannot be seen now. The remains of about 14 people were found in it, piled up on a stone floor beneath a wooden, tent-like mortuary house, which had been covered over with a mound of chalk.

This massive ditch near Wheathampstead, known as the Devil's Dyke, was probably part of the defences of Caswallon's base, attacked by Julius Caesar in 54 BC.

Waulud's Bank, Bedfordshire

TL 062246, in a public park at Leagrave, NW of Luton. The River Lea rises inside an enclosure surrounded by a low, horseshoe-shaped bank of chalk, with a ditch originally 30 ft (9 m) wide and 8 ft (2.4 m) deep, constructed in late Neolithic times. Many flint arrowheads were found here, suggesting that the place had been attacked. It may have been a henge like the one at Marden in Wiltshire.

West Wycombe, Buckinghamshire

SP 828949. The church, a landmark for miles around, stands inside a small Iron Age fort, with ramparts up to 11 ft (3.3 m) high, covered with trees. Sir Francis Dashwood, of West Wycombe Park and Hellfire Club fame, built the mausoleum on the SE side in the 1760s. The caves under the hill are medieval and artificial.

Wheathampstead

On the E outskirts, commanding a ford over the River Lea, is a formidable earthwork called the **Devil's Dyke** TL 183133 (*National Trust*), a ditch 40 ft (12 m) deep and 90 ft (27 m) wide, running between 2 banks. To the E is a similar earthwork called the **Slad**. These may have been part of the defences of a 90-acre (36-ha) stronghold here, the principal base of Caswallon, the Catuvellaunian king who led the British resistance to Julius Caesar. An alternative theory sees these massive works as outlying defences of the new capital which, after Caesar's departure, Caswallon constructed at Prae Wood, above a ford over the River Ver, to the W of St Albans, where the Roman town of Verulamium was afterwards built. **Beech Bottom Dyke** TL 155092, 1 mile (1.6 km) N of the centre of St Albans, between A6 and B651, is 29 ft (9 m) deep and 90 ft (27 m) wide, and was presumably an outwork protecting the Prae Wood position.

Whiteleaf Barrow, Buckinghamshire

SP 822040, 1 mile (1.6 km) NE of Princes Risborough, off the Ridgeway Path. An overgrown barrow of about 2500 BC stands on a ridge above the Whiteleaf Cross, which was first cut in the Middle Ages. Inside were found the left foot and a single tooth of a man of about 35 who had suffered from arthritis. The rest of his bones were in the forecourt. Were they left there after being brought out for a ritual? It seems very strange.

JULIUS CAESAR IN ENGLAND

In August of the year 55 BC, Gaius Julius Caesar was 47 years old. Tall, bald, daring, vigorous, superbly efficient and intensely ambitious, one of the most formidable military commanders who ever lived and a notable orator and writer, he had reduced the Celtic tribes of France to an uneasy obedience to Rome. He now looked across the Channel, partly to prevent the Celts in England stirring up trouble in France and partly to heighten his own prestige at home. In 55 he made an armed reconnaissance, landing in Kent with 10,000 men and soon leaving again. In 54, in the month that would afterwards be named July in his honour, he crossed the Channel in force with 25,000 legionaries and 2000 cavalry in 800 ships, and landed near Walmer in Kent.

The British war leader was Caswallon (Cassivellaunus to the Romans), the king of the Catuvellauni people in Hertfordshire. He seems to have been recognized by the other rulers and chieftains of southern England as their high king. The Romans advanced to the British stronghold of Bigbury Camp, to the west of Canterbury, where the

Statue of Julius Caesar, in Rome. Having carried out a reconnaissance in force in 55 BC, he invaded south-eastern England the following year.

Seventh Legion stormed the defences. They then had to retreat to their base on the coast to repair their ships, which had been badly damaged in a sudden easterly gale. Marching westwards once more, the Romans were severely hampered by the hit-and-run tactics of the British cavalry and war chariots, but they crossed the Medway and reached the Thames. Fording the river, perhaps where Brentford is now, the Roman legions forced their way on, probably through the Colne Valley and by modern Denham, Rickmansworth and Watford to Caswallon's own great citadel and capital at Wheathampstead.

By this time many of the British sub-kings were seeking to make peace. Caswallon and his warriors fought on, bravely and skilfully, but they were no match for Caesar and his troops, who took the stronghold in a determined assault. Caswallon escaped and sent messages to chieftains in Kent, who attacked the Roman base-camp there, but were beaten off. This last throw having failed, Caswallon made a treaty with Caesar, who took his numerous hostages and his army back to France to face a fierce Celtic rebellion. Perhaps Caesar intended to return to England and conquer it one day, but he never did. He was assassinated in Rome on the fateful Ides of March 10 years later. Caswallon long outlived him, dying in about 20 BC.

Caesar had special ships built for his invasion fleet in 54 BC, lower and wider than usual, for carrying cavalry horses and heavy cargo. On the way over the wind failed and the Roman soldiers had to row hard to reach the landing place.

Part of the nature reserve at Wicken Fen in Cambridgeshire, where, as early as the Bronze Age, fenmen constructed artificial trackways through the marshes.

THE EASTERN COUNTIES
NORFOLK, SUFFOLK, CAMBRIDGESHIRE, ESSEX

CONCEALED beneath the golf course near the holiday camp at Clacton on Sea is a place where some of the earliest human beings in Britain were to be found about 250,000 years ago. There was no North Sea then and they camped on the bank of a river. A spearhead they had made of yew wood was found there, the world's oldest wooden implement. Traces of other Stone Age hunters have been found in Norfolk and Suffolk.

Much later on, Neolithic and Bronze Age farmers lived in the valleys of the Cam, Ouse, Nene and other rivers, in the fen country round Mildenhall, in the Ipswich region and on the heaths of the Breckland, around Thetford, where some of their barrows have survived. Not a great deal is left to see on the ground, but an exceptionally interesting place to visit is Grime's Graves in Norfolk. The prehistoric flint mines there are the only ones in England which have been opened to the public.

Grime's Graves is not far from the Icknield Way, the prehistoric route from Norfolk to Salisbury Plain, which was a cattle drovers' road until the nineteenth century. Today the A11 and A505 roads follow much of its course. Another prehistoric track, the Peddars' Way, runs northward from Ixworth in Suffolk. North of Castle Acre in Norfolk it was turned into a Roman road and runs straight as an arrow most of the way to the coast, with barrows along it. The draining of the fens did not begin until Roman times, but long before, in the Bronze Age, causeways built of faggots were laid through the wilderness of the marshes. Prehistoric people were far more resourceful than they are generally given credit for.

Magnificent treasure hoards of Iron Age gold ornaments were found at Snettisham in Norfolk in the late 1940s and at Ipswich in 1968, and can be seen in the Norwich Castle and Ipswich museums. Also surviving majestically from Celtic times are parts of the great earthworks which protected Colchester against attack when it was the capital of Cunobelin, who ruled all south-east England before the Romans came. Long afterwards he was immortalized by Shakespeare, as Cymbeline.

Museums of interest
University Museum of Archaeology and Anthropology, Cambridge; Colchester and Essex Museum, Colchester Castle; Ipswich Museum; Norwich Castle Museum; Ancient House Museum, Thetford.

Neolithic pottery bowl from Mildenhall in Suffolk, where the early farmers settled in the fen country.

This magnificent torc, or neck ring, of gold mixed with silver, dates from about 50 BC and was found at Snettisham in Norfolk. The eight twisted strands are soldered into heavy terminals, which are carved in relief.

PLACES TO VISIT

Ambresbury Banks, Essex
TL 438004, in Epping Forest, 2 miles (3.2 km) SW of Epping, on S side of A11. The fort has a single bank and ditch, the bank up to 7 ft (2.1 m) high, enclosing about 11 acres (4.5 ha). A stream inside the S end of the fort gives it a water supply. According to one theory, it was here that

Queen Boudicca (Boadicea) of the Iceni fought the Romans in AD 61. To the SW, also close to A11, is **Loughton Camp** TQ 418975, another hillfort with its own stream inside it. It is protected by a single rampart and a ditch up to 8 ft (2.4 m) deep and 45 ft (13.5 m) wide in places.

Ambresbury Banks is a low-lying Iron Age fort in Epping Forest, traditionally the scene of the battle between the Romans and the British rebels led by Queen Boadicea in AD 61.

Arminghall, Norfolk

TG 240060, on the outskirts of Norwich. A henge stood here in 3250 BC and was discovered from the air in 1929, but there is little to see now. A horseshoe of 8 huge oak posts, weighing 7 tons each, perhaps painted or carved, and perhaps supporting a roof, stood inside an outer bank. The henge was apparently aligned on the midwinter sunset.

Colchester, Essex

The area called Lexden Park stands on the site of the capital of King Cunobelin. The town was called 'the war-god's stronghold' (Camulodunum in Latin) and covered about 12 acres (5 ha), including the townspeople's fields and pastures as well as their houses. It was close to the sea and did a thriving import-export trade, bringing in wine, oil and luxuries from the Continent, and Cunobelin struck gold, silver and bronze coins at his mint here. The town was protected on the N and E by the River Colne and on the S by the River Roman. The gap in the W between the two rivers was defended by a complicated system of formidable earthworks, 12 ft (3.6 m) high, with V-shaped ditches in front of them, close to 12 ft (3.6 m) deep and 70 ft (21 m) wide at the top. Stretches of these defences can

CLAUDIUS AND CARADOC

After Julius Caesar's expedition in 54 BC, Rome left the Britons in peace for almost a hundred years. Internecine wars flared and flickered among the kings and chiefs of southern England, however, and the descendants of Caswallon extended their territory and influence. The most powerful of them, Cunobelin, took the whole south-east in his grip. Cunobelin died in about AD 40. His sons, one of whom was Caradoc – the Romans called him Caratacus – launched an attack on a petty king named Verica, who fled to Rome and asked the Emperor Claudius to intervene.

Claudius took the opportunity and assembled an invasion force of four legions and auxiliaries, about 40,000 men. Commanded by a general named Aulus Plautius, they sailed from Boulogne in the summer of AD 43 and landed at Richborough in Kent. Caradoc opposed them at the Medway, somewhere near Rochester, where a desperate struggle lasted for 2 days. The Roman soldiers then succeeded in swimming the river in full armour and the British were forced back. Many British chieftains were more afraid of Caradoc than of the Romans and supported or did not resist the invasion, but the legions had to beat off fierce attacks from Caradoc and his men before they could cross the Thames.

At this point Claudius arrived to take command in person, bringing with him reinforcements including elephants to oppose the British cavalry and chariots. He won a battle north of the Thames and entered Colchester, which he made the capital of the new Roman province of Britannia. After 16 days in Britain he returned to Rome to celebrate a magnificent triumph. Caradoc escaped to Wales, but was

Bust of the Emperor Claudius, from the Vatican Museum, Rome. The stammering Claudius came to England in AD 43 to lead his conquering army in person.

eventually betrayed to the Romans and sent to Rome in chains. Astounded by the grandeur of the city, he is said to have asked why the Romans wanted a poor place like Britain when they had so much already. Claudius treated him kindly and he ended his life in honoured captivity in Rome.

Part of the underground workings in the Neolithic flint mines at Grime's Graves in Norfolk. Shafts were dug 40 ft (12 m) deep with simple antler picks, and galleries radiated from the foot of each shaft.

This bronze boar was one of the objects found in the Lexden Tumulus in Colchester, a rich grave of the early first century AD which was probably the tomb of a Celtic king. Another find was a pendant made from a silver coin of the Emperor Augustus (above). They are both in the Colchester and Essex Museum.

still be seen, and the **Lexden Earthworks** TL 963240 are in the charge of the *Dept of the Environment*.

The **Lexden Tumulus** is a circular mound, 6 ft (1.8 m) high and 75 ft (23 m) in diameter, on private property in the gardens of 30 and 36 Fitzwalter Road but visible from the street. It contained rich grave goods, now in the Colchester Museum, including the remains of silver-studded body armour, a robe embroidered in gold, bronze statuettes, wine jars and a silver medallion of the Emperor Augustus, for the dead man's use in the next world. It is possible that this was the grave of Cunobelin himself, but considered more likely that it was the tomb of a rather earlier king.

Grime's Graves, Norfolk

TL 818898, *Dept of the Environment*, in the Breckland, 3 miles (4.8 km) NE of Brandon. The flint mines, in a stretch of heath among pine woods, date from about 3000 BC and constitute one of the most fascinating prehistoric sites in the country. The area is humped and hummocked with grassed-over spoil mounds and more than 300 filled-in shafts. In the N part of the site the flint seam ran near the surface and was quarried out and dug from small pits, up to 14 ft (4.2 m) deep. To the S, where the seam went deeper, the miners dug shafts as much as 40 ft (12 m) down and 30 ft (9 m) wide at the top. Cramped galleries, some only 2 to 3 ft (1 m) high, radiate from the foot of each

shaft. Climbing down into one of these shafts today is a memorable experience (a torch is useful).

The flint was dug out with antler picks and flint and stone axes and hammers, and hoisted up to the surface in skin bags or baskets on ropes. Wooden or rope ladders

This small, obese figure in chalk, only 4½ in (11.5 cm) high, was found in an abandoned shaft at Grime's Graves. It probably represents the Earth Mother.

were probably used for access. Pinewood torches and chalk cups filled with fat and a floating wick provided light down below and have left sooty stains on the gallery roofs. In one shaft where the seam had run out the miners put a little, squat, bulging female figurine, presumably a figure of the Earth Mother, with some fertility symbols, apparently to stimulate her to 'give birth' to more flint. It is thought that perhaps 20 men worked one shaft, half of them below ground and the others hauling the flint up to the surface and chipping it into rough axeheads. One of them scratched a picture of a stag on a bit of flint and an antler pick found here still had on it a chalky fingerprint left by a miner of thousands of years ago. The flint-knapping industry, incidentally, continued at nearby Brandon for many centuries, until quite recently. There is a small collection of finds at the site, and Norwich Castle Museum has an interesting display.

Wallbury Camp, Essex

TL 493178, 2 miles (3.2 km) s of Bishop's Stortford. Above the River Stour is a tree-covered fort on a spur with ramparts rising 14 ft (4.2 m) above the bottom of the ditch.

MINERS AND SMITHS: PREHISTORIC INDUSTRY

So accustomed are we to thinking of our prehistoric forebears as primitive and savage that it can come as a shock to discover that they had quarries and mines. From at least 4000 BC commercial axe factories were in operation – in Cornwall and subsequently in Cumbria, Wales and Ireland – at sites where suitable rock to make efficient edged tools could be quarried. The products were rough-cut tools which were carried all over the country by traders, to be finished and honed by the buyers.

The same thing is true of the products of the flint mines, at places like Grime's Graves or Cissbury Ring on the South Downs. With antler picks and stone hammers, shafts were sunk deep into the chalk, and miners crouching sweatily in low tunnels created networks of underground galleries like complicated mole-runs. The miners may have formed something of a separate caste, set apart by their special skills and the dangers they faced.

At some time in the third millennium BC the craft of the metal-smith first came to Britain. Smiths probably had a magical mystique about them from the very beginning, for their operations are awesome and uncanny to the uninitiated. Wandering smiths travelled the length and breadth of the land, singly or in small groups. They carried their tools and moulds and a few ingots of bronze and they would pause for a few days at a settlement to set up a furnace and meet the local orders before moving on.

No one knows whether it was armed invaders who first brought iron weapons and tools to Britain, or merchants or smiths who came to settle here. Iron ore was smelted in ovens heated by charcoal, and the main iron producing regions were the Forest of Dean and the Weald, but iron was found in far more places than copper or tin. The travelling smith was replaced by the local blacksmith, who stayed in his village all his life. A magical aura clung to him all the same, well into modern times.

This artist's reconstruction shows a wandering smith of the Bronze Age with some of his equipment.

The nature reserve at Wicken Fen preserves a stretch of fen country in as close to its natural, pre-Roman state as can be found in England.

Warham Camp was built by the Iceni, probably not long before the Roman invasion. It was the Iceni under Boadicea who later rebelled against Roman rule.

Wandlebury, Cambridgeshire

TL 493534, beside A604, 5 miles (8.0 km) SE of Cambridge. This circular hillfort is in a delightful wooded area, owned by the Cambridge Preservation Society and open to the public, on the low range of the Gog Magog Hills. To the E

Wandlebury hillfort, near Cambridge, is in a wooded area in the curiously named Gog Magog Hills.

is a Roman road, the Via Devana. Gog and Magog are traditionally the names of giants, and the Cambridge antiquary, T.C. Lethbridge, believed he had discovered three gigantic figures of Celtic deities cut into the chalk here – though other archaeologists were unable to agree with him. The hillfort covers about 15 acres (6 ha), defended by 2 main ramparts with a ditch between them, with the original entrance in the SE. Parts of the defences were destroyed in the eighteenth century, when the Earl of Godolphin landscaped the grounds of his house here. His famous stallion, the Godolphin Arabian, was buried here in 1753.

Warham Camp, Norfolk

TF 044409, 3 miles (4.8 km) SE of Wells-next-the-Sea. Impressive fort with double ramparts about 9 ft (2.7 m) high, above the River Stiffkey. It was presumably built by the Iceni not long before the coming of the Romans. Most of the gaps in the ramparts are modern.

Wicken Fen, Cambridgeshire

TL 559707, *National Trust*, 10 miles (16 km) NE of Cambridge, S of B1085. The nature reserve here preserves an area of the fens in their natural, undrained state, with rich plant, bird and insect life, in as close to their pre-Roman condition as exists anywhere in England. Part of the reserve is open to the general public, with a walking route of about 2 miles (3.2 km).

Mam Tor, seen from Hollins Cross. This Derbyshire mountain is crowned by a formidable hillfort which may date from late in the Bronze Age.

THE NORTH MIDLANDS
CHESHIRE, SHROPSHIRE, STAFFORDSHIRE, DERBYSHIRE, NOTTINGHAMSHIRE, LEICESTERSHIRE, LINCOLNSHIRE

THE caves in the narrow gorge of Cresswell Crags on the border of Derbyshire and Nottinghamshire have engaging names: Mother Grundy's Parlour, Robin Hood's Cave, Pin Hole Cave and the rest. The chance discovery of a fossilized mammoth's tooth in 1870 led to thorough exploration of these caves. Digging down through the thick layers of debris and dust on the cave floors revealed that they were among the oldest inhabited places in Britain. They were occupied by Neanderthal families more than 40,000 years ago. After the end of the Ice Age, about 12,000 years ago, human beings known to archaeologists as Cresswellians, after this site, hunted reindeer, horse and bison here and also produced the earliest crude pieces of art in Britain – though nothing has been discovered in this country to compare with the superb cave art of France and Spain.

The most famous prehistoric monument in the North Midlands is the stone circle of Arbor Low in lonely, windswept moorland in the Peak District. Not far to the north and south are a number of robbed and devastated Neolithic tombs, and a great Bronze Age sacred centre and burying ground can be visited on Stanton Moor.

Trade routes ran across the Peak area in very early times, connecting East Anglia with North Wales and the Lake District. Another route came from Ireland across the sea to Anglesey and by Oswestry to Shrewsbury and the Severn valley, leading down to the south and south-west. The Severn itself would have been used by traders and travellers in canoes and coracles. There were many farms and hamlets in the Shropshire lowlands and in the south of the country: Clun is believed to be one of the oldest settlements in England.

The most prominent prehistoric objects in Shropshire today, however, are the Iron Age hillforts. Almost every hill in the west of the county is topped with one. The Celtic people whom the Romans called Cornovii occupied what are now Cheshire, Shropshire and Staffordshire, and their principal base may have been the hillfort on the Wrekin. Further to the east, in the more heavily settled and cultivated lowland areas of the Midlands, comparatively little has survived the toll of the years, but there is a concentration of Neolithic long barrows on the Lincolnshire Wolds.

Museums of interest
Buxton Museum & Art Gallery; Clun Town Trust Museum; Jewry Wall Museum, Leicester; Lincoln City and County Museum.

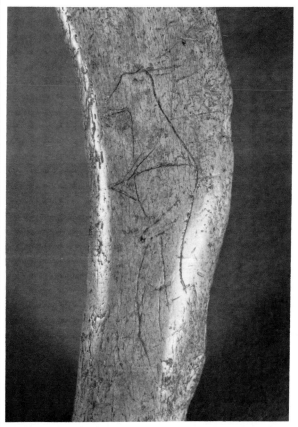

The crude carving on this piece of bone from Pin Hole Cave may be about 12,000 years old. Only about 1½ in (3.8 cm) high, it seems to represent a Stone Age priest-magician, wearing an animal mask and holding a bow.

PLACES TO VISIT

Arbor Low, Derbyshire

SK 160636 *Dept of the Environment*, on Middleton Moor, 3 miles (4.8 km) W of Middleton. This henge, 1230 ft (374 m) up in isolated country, was built soon after 3000 BC. It has an oval bank, 250 ft (83 m) across at its widest and standing on average 7 ft (2.1 m) high, with entrances at N and S. Inside this is a broad ditch, from which the builders laboriously dug out 50,000 cubic feet of limestone to make the bank. Inside this again are 40-odd limestone blocks lying in an egg-shaped ring. Whether they ever stood upright is uncertain. At the centre is a cove, facing SW. Just to the E of this was discovered a male skeleton surrounded by stones. There is a round barrow by the S entrance and a much bigger one to the SW, 16 ft (4.8 m) high and called **Gib Hill**, from an eighteenth-century gibbet that stood here. Both barrows contained cremated bodies in stone cists. A low curving bank runs towards Gib Hill from the henge, which was the main ritual centre for the area in late Neolithic times.

Bridestones, Cheshire

SJ 906622, 3 miles (4.8 km) E of Congleton on the Cheshire–Staffordshire border. This Neolithic tomb takes its name from the local story that a Viking chieftain and his English bride were buried here, but in reality dates back to 2500 BC or earlier. It was originally covered by a mound 300 ft (91 m) long, running E/W. At the E end are the remains of a forecourt.

Bully Hills, Lincolnshire

TF 330827, 3 miles (4.8 km) S of Louth. Bronze Age group

Gib Hill is a large Bronze Age round barrow near the Arbor Low circle. A gibbet once stood on top of it, hence its name.

of 7 bowl barrows in line, up to 80 ft (24 m) in diameter and 10 ft (3 m) high.

The Bulwarks, Leicestershire

SK 406234, at Breedon on the Hill. The village clusters round this Iron Age hillfort, much damaged by quarrying but still impressive.

Burrough Hill, Leicestershire

SK 761119, 5 miles (8 km) S of Melton Mowbray. This fine hillfort on a steep hill, covering 12 acres (5 ha), with a massive rampart and ditch, is a popular beauty spot. Constructed about 150 BC, it may have been a centre of the Coritani, the Celtic people of this area. The entrance at the SE had a cobbled roadway and stone guard-houses.

Arbor Low stone circle, on windswept Derbyshire moorland. About 40 blocks of local limestone were placed here soon after 3000 BC, in a ring surrounded by a bank and ditch.

Close-up view of one of the eroded limestone slabs at Arbor Low. Whether the stones originally stood upright is uncertain, but they may have been propped up with smaller stones.

Two tall pillars loom up at the E end of the Bridestones, near Congleton, a ruined Neolithic burial chamber which was once covered by a mound of earth 300 ft (91 m) long.

The fort on Burrough Hill is protected by the steep sides of the hill itself and by a rampart and ditch.

Bury Ditches, Shropshire

SO 327836, 2 miles (3.2 km) NE of Clun, in the woods near Lower Down. This hillfort has no fewer than 5 ramparts at the NE. There are elaborate entrances at the NE and SW.

Bury Walls, Shropshire

SJ 576275, 4 miles (6.4 km) E of Wem. An impressive promontory fort on a steep spur, covering $13\frac{1}{2}$ acres (5.5 ha). On the N are two ramparts and ditches, the inner one looming up over 30 ft (9 m) above its ditch. The NE entrance was cut deep into rock.

Caer Caradoc, Shropshire

SO 477953, 2 miles (3.2 km) NE of Church Stretton. This fort on a steep ridge above the Roman Watling Street is protected by rock outcrops as well as a rampart and ditch. A track was constructed up the E side of the hill to the fort's SE gateway, where there was a guard-house. This is

Caer Caradoc fort, above Church Stretton, where the British resistance hero Caradoc is said to have made his brave last stand against the Romans. The honour is also claimed by another Caer Caradoc, near Clun.

one of the strongholds traditionally claimed as the place where the British chieftain Caradoc made a last defiant but hopeless stand against the Romans, and he is said to have hidden in the cave on the w side of the hill. Fleeing to the Brigantes people in the north, he was handed over to the Romans by Queen Cartimandua.

Across the valley is the 10-mile (16-km) moorland plateau of the Long Mynd (rhyming with 'pinned'), full of heather, beauty spots and delightful walks. The ancient track along the top, the Port Way, may have been used by prehistoric axe traders, and there are numerous barrows, earthworks and enclosures to be seen.

Caer Caradoc, Shropshire

SO 310758, ½ mile (804 m) s of Chapel Lawn, s of Clun. This impressive small fort with double and triple ramparts is also named for Caradoc and is an alternative site of his last stand (which may actually have occurred in Wales). To the N, 1½ miles (2.4 km) away, are the remains of the **Pen Y Wern** stone circle, on a 1250-ft (380-m) hill.

THE FOREST PRIMEVAL

The landscape of England is the child of two parents – geology and man. Our scenery has been largely created by thousands of years of human activity – farming, building, mining, quarrying – which began far in the past with the slow, steady destruction of the blanket of primeval forest which once swathed the country. The forest grew in the wake of the retreating Ice Age glaciers. As temperatures rose, trees strode northwards, with pines and birches in the van. By about 7000 BC lowland England was

Cannock Chase still retains its native oak, birch and heather, and its wild deer. Much of England's primeval woodland had been cleared by the first century AD, but large patches of forest survived, and were preserved for breeding and hunting game in the Middle Ages.

covered by deciduous forest dominated by lime, oak, alder and elm, interspersed with ash and beech, maple and hornbeam, elder and holly, ivy and mistletoe. On higher ground grew forests of pine, birch and hazel.

The trees of the primeval forest were taller and straighter than those of today. Parts of the forest were dense and thickly tangled with undergrowth, parts were wet and swampy, but there were probably also areas of open glade, browsed by deer and wild ox. Through the woodlands moved the nomadic Middle Stone Age hunters with their bows, traps, nets and canoes, often camping beside streams and lakes.

Late in the Mesolithic period there is evidence of patches of forest being cleared by burning. The process was vigorously continued by the Neolithic farmers, whose cattle and sheep grazed on the cleared patches and prevented the forest from re-establishing itself. Pollen analysis has shown that substantial areas of woodland were cleared between about 4500 and 3000 BC. Large stretches of open downland and heath emerged – such as the South Downs, Salisbury Plain and the Breckland in East Anglia. Oddly enough, in the centuries around 3500 BC there was a marked decline in the number of elm trees, perhaps the result of an epidemic of Dutch Elm disease, like the recent outbreak.

Forest clearance forged steadily on during the Bronze and Iron Ages. The destruction of the birch cover in northern England caused erosion of the soil, and human zeal in destroying woodland is believed to have been one of the main causes of the formation of peat. By the time the Romans came, the once continuous blanket of forest had been reduced to shreds and patches. However, some of the patches were still extremely large, forming such great forests as the Weald, the Forest of Dean and the forests of the Midlands, including Arden, Clun, Sherwood, Charnwood, Needwood and Cannock Chase.

Castle Ditch, Cheshire

SJ 553695. Fort on Eddisbury Hill, 2 miles (3.2 km) NE of Congleton, first occupied in the second century BC, when it was protected by a palisade. The ramparts were built later and the fort was dismantled by the Romans, but occupied again much later, in the tenth century AD.

Castle Ring, Staffordshire

SK 045128, 3 miles (4.8 km) S of Rugeley. This five-sided hillfort, commandingly placed among the woodland and heath of Cannock Chase, is a well-known beauty spot. On the S and SE it is defended by 5 banks and 4 ditches.

Cresswell Crags, Derbyshire

SL 538743, 3 miles (4.8 km) E of Clowne. The caves in this limestone gorge are among the oldest homes in Britain, occupied at intervals from Neanderthal to Neolithic times. Carvings on animal bones were found here, including an engraving of a horse's head, another of a reindeer and a tiny sketch of a dancing man in an animal mask, engraved on a piece of reindeer bone, perhaps representing a priest-magician performing a fertility ritual. For long periods the caves were the dens of hyenas, and the remains of numerous animals were found in them, including cave lion, bear and woolly rhino. There is an interesting visitor centre here. The caves themselves can be looked into, but not explored.

The impressive hillfort of Castle Ring in Cannock Chase is protected by multiple banks and ditches.

Five Wells, Derbyshire

SK 124711, on Taddington Moor, 1 mile (1.6 km) NW of Taddington, in the Peak District. Remains of a dozen or more bodies were found, with flint tools and pottery, in this ruined Neolithic tomb, whose capstone and covering mound have long since gone. There were two burial chambers, backing on to each other and approached by passages from the W and E.

Giant's Hill, Lincolnshire

TF 429712, 1 mile (1.6 km) NW of Skendlebury, W of

A sweeping view from the hillfort on Mam Tor, which is also known as Shivering Mountain because its layers of shale and grit fall away in frequent landslides. The edge can be seen in the foreground.

A1028. Before the main barrow here was built, in about 3100 BC, a wooden mortuary house was constructed, 189 ft (57.5 m) long by 37 ft (11.2 m) wide. Inside, bones from 8 corpses were piled on a chalk platform. At the NW end of the barrow stood 8 tall posts, presumably one for each of the dead. Bones of oxen, sheep and deer were found in the covering mound, which is 210 ft (64 m) long.

Helsby Hill, Cheshire

SJ 491752, *National Trust*, ½ mile (804 m) S of Helsby. The Trust property includes a promontory fort with fine views over the Mersey and to the Welsh mountains.

Honington Camp, Lincolnshire

SK 954424, 1 mile (1.6 km) SE of Honington. Small Iron Age fort above the River Witham, with double ramparts and ditches surrounded by an outer bank.

Kinver, Staffordshire

SO 835832, *National Trust*, 4 miles (6.4 km) W of Stourbridge. Commanding one of the finest views in the Midlands from the N end of Kinver Ridge, this promontory fort is protected by a bank rising to 15 ft (4.5 m). Nearby are the caves of Holy Austin Rock, which were used as houses down to the nineteenth century.

Maiden Castle, Cheshire

SJ 497529, promontory fort of the second century BC on the NW side of Bickerton Hill, N of Malpas, protected by steep hillsides. On the SE a cobbled entrance way led through the ramparts to a wooden gate.

Mam Tor, Derbyshire

SK 128838, *National Trust*, 1½ miles (2.4 km) W of Castleton. This 1700-ft (517-m) mountain, whose name might perhaps preserve the name of a prehistoric mother goddess, is crowned by a formidable fort, possibly dating from the late Bronze Age, with a rampart 30 ft (9 m) above the ditch. Inside are 2 Bronze Age round barrows and numerous circular hut platforms. The fort once covered 16 acres (7 ha), but parts of it have slipped down the hillside. Several spectacular caves in this area with beautiful formations, stalactites and stalagmites, are open to visitors: Blue John Caverns, Peak Cavern, Treak Cliff Cavern, Speedwell Cavern.

Mitchell's Fold, Shropshire

SO 304983, *Dept of the Environment*, to N of Corndon Hill, 5 miles (8 km) NW of Lydham. In a fine mountain setting with a sweeping view over Wales, this Bronze Age stone circle has 10 stones still standing, from 2 ft to 6 ft (0.6 to

The stone circle of Mitchell's Fold on its remote hillside in Shropshire commands a beautiful prospect of Wales. The tallest stones stand 6 ft (1.8 m) high.

1.8 m) tall, and a diameter of 75 ft (23 m). There may have been a stone at the centre originally. There was an axe factory at Cwm Mawr to the S, whose products were distributed throughout the Midlands. In marshy moorland to the NE is the **Hemford** or **Hoar Stone** circle SO 324999, of 38 low stones, with a stone at the centre and 2 barrows close by.

Nine Stones Circle, Derbyshire

SK 225625, 3 miles (4.8 km) S of Bakewell, on Harthill Moor. Only 4 massive stones are left of this circle, the tallest being 7 ft (2.1 m) high. The stones are also known as the Grey Ladies and it is said that on moonlit nights they bestir themselves into a lumbering dance. Nearby is the small hillfort of **Castle Ring** SK 221628.

Old Oswestry fort was a powerful British stronghold before the Romans came and was occupied again

after they left. Like many other hillforts, it was enlarged and strengthened over several centuries.

The remains of a cist, or stone coffin, in one of the numerous burial cairns on Stanton Moor, an important Bronze Age sacred site in Derbyshire.

Old Oswestry, Shropshire

SJ 296310, *Dept of the Environment*, 1 mile (1.6 km) N of Oswestry. This superb hillfort has massive and complicated defences, with entrances at the E and W. The hill was occupied in about 500 BC by people who lived in round wooden houses. Later there was a settlement of round stone houses here, and in about 250 BC 2 earth ramparts, faced with stone, were built to defend it. Later 2 more ramparts were added, and later still 2 immense outer banks were thrown up round the base of the hill. The stronghold was reoccupied by the British after the Roman period. Running through the fort is Wat's Dyke, an earthwork constructed in the eighth century AD as the boundary between Anglo-Saxon Mercia and the Welsh.

Stanton Moor, Derbyshire

This area to the NE of Birchover, partly *National Trust*, has been described as 'like a lost world'. About 2 miles (3.2 km) long by 1 mile (1.6 km) wide, it contains a remarkable concentration of cairns, dating from about 2000 BC, and was evidently a venerated site. **Doll Tor** SK 238628 is a circle of 4 standing and 2 fallen stones, joined by a ring of smaller stones, with a cairn on the E. The **Nine Ladies** circle SK 249635 (*Dept of the Environment*), consists of smallish stones surrounded by a low bank and a modern stone wall. Nearby to the SW is the **King Stone**, a solitary outlier 3 ft (1 m) high. Tradition has it that the 'nine ladies' were turned to stone to punish them for dancing on the sabbath day: the King Stone was their fiddler. There are many other solitary pillars standing on the moor, but they are natural rock formations and some of them, such as the Cork Stone, have been fitted with metal ladders to aid climbing. Many of the finds from the moor are in the private Heathcote Museum in Birchover.

Thor's Cave, Staffordshire

SK 098549. This cave with a huge gaping entrance above the River Manifold, NW of Ashbourne, was occupied during the Old Stone Age and again for 500 years or so after about 200 BC.

The four surviving stones of the Nine Stones or Grey Ladies circle on Harthill Moor in Derbyshire. The tallest one is 7 ft (2.1 m) high, with over half as much below ground.

Titterstone Clee Hill, Shropshire

SO 592779, E of Bitterley. A very large fort, of 71 acres (29 ha), stands on top of this 1750-ft (533-m) hill, with splendid views, defended by a single rampart of earth and rubble. There are traces of hut circles on the E side. Coal was mined here until the end of the nineteenth century and the fort has recently been damaged by quarrying.

Nordy Bank is a small fort on a spur of the Clee Hills in Shropshire, which well into this century retained its ancient reputation as the haunt of evil spirits and witches.

The turf maze at Wing in Leicestershire, possibly laid out in the Middle Ages on a much older ceremonial site.

The whale-backed hump of the Wrekin is the best-known landmark in Shropshire. On top is an Iron Age stronghold. The sides of the hill were artificially steepened by the builders to strengthen the defences.

To the N is Brown Clee Hill, 1800 ft (548 m). There is another hillfort here, **Nordy Bank** SO 576847, on a spur above Clee St Margaret, with a single bank and ditch, and 2 more, **Abdon Burf** and **Clee Burf**, which have been wrecked by quarrying. According to the sixteenth-century writer John Leland, 'Clee Hills be holy in Shropshire', and the hills were reputedly a haunt of witches and evil spirits well into this century.

Wet Withins, Derbyshire

SK 225790, 1 mile (1.6 km) SW of Hathersage, on Eyam Moor (Eyam is pronounced to rhyme with 'gleam'). Two concentric rings of stones here surround a burial, with cairns nearby.

Wing, Leicestershire

SK 895028. The famous turf maze here is 40 ft (12 m) in diameter. It may have been laid out in medieval times on a much older ritual site.

The Wrekin, Shropshire

SJ 630083. The fort on top of this celebrated 1350-ft (411-m) hill, the best-known landmark in the county, may have been the principal stronghold of the Cornovii before the Romans moved their capital to a new centre at Wroxeter. First fortified in about 400 BC and later strengthened, it has entrances at the E and W, which were protected by stone guard-houses. At the SW are the remains of a Bronze Age round barrow.

THE GAME OF TROY

Only a few of the old turf-cut mazes survive in England. There were once many more of them and they were still being made in Wales in the eighteenth century. Hedge-mazes, like the famous one at Hampton Court in London, were constructed solely for amusement, but the turf-cut kind have a much longer history, connected with ritual. They were often called Troys, Troy Towns or Walls of Troy. During the Middle Ages they were used for dances, games and processions, which may have preserved a tradition of maze rituals going back ultimately to prehistoric times. There is fragmentary and tantalisingly enigmatic evidence of the maze as a sacred pattern in the ancient world, connected with labyrinthine, spiralling religious dances and linked with fertility and funerary rituals, because the heart of the maze was believed to hold the key to the inner secret of life and death. In prehistoric England mazes may have been marked out on the ground for dancers to tread the winding path to the centre and return again, symbolizing death and rebirth.

The link with Troy seems to be a legacy from the Romans. In the *Aeneid* Virgil describes Trojan funeral games, including an intricate display by horsemen riding in intertwining circular patterns, which he compares to the famous Cretan labyrinth – the maze in which lurked the Minotaur, the monster, part man and part bull. Other Roman writers mention 'the game of Troy', and when Roman administrators and soldiers came to England they may have given the name to maze rituals which they found being performed here.

What Shakespeare called 'the quaint mazes in the wanton green' (A Midsummer Night's Dream) may have been constructed originally for prehistoric rituals. Illustrated here, from left to right, are : Shepherd's Race or Robin Hood's Race at Sneinton, Notts, ploughed up in 1799; turf maze at Hilton, Cambridgeshire, with an obelisk at the centre; Troy Town, Pimperne, Dorset, ploughed up in 1730; Troy Town at Somerton, Oxfordshire.

One of the Devil's Arrows, three enormous standing monoliths at Boroughbridge in North Yorkshire. The grooves are believed to have been cut by wind and rain over the centuries.

YORKSHIRE AND THE NORTH-EAST

NORTHUMBERLAND, TYNE & WEAR, DURHAM, CLEVELAND, THE YORKSHIRES, HUMBERSIDE

THE richest Middle Stone Age discovery in Britain was made in this area, at Star Carr, south of Scarborough, where 10,000 years ago a nomadic hunting group of 20 to 25 people had a camp beside a lake. There is nothing there now, but the site is marked on the Ordnance Survey maps, TA 027810, and some of the finds are in Scarborough Museum. The group hunted deer, wild ox and wild boar, and they owned tame or semi-tame dogs. They had antlered headdresses made from the skulls of stags, which they presumably wore in ritual dances and religio-magical ceremonies. England was not yet separated from the Continent and groups like this used dugout canoes to cross the marshes where the North Sea is today.

Farmers moved into the north-east before 3000 BC and settled down to clear the land and grow their crops generation by generation, on into the ages of bronze and iron. There were once many barrows on the Yorkshire Wolds, though most of them have been ploughed up, and long earthworks which were possibly the corrals and enclosures of the great horse ranches which were flourishing here when the Romans arrived. They belonged to a Celtic tribe, the Parisi, who came from France, where they left their name to Paris. Their aristocrats were buried in state with their war chariots, and one of these chariot burials is on display at Hull Museum.

Further north, among the heather and bracken of the solitary North York Moors, are thousands of barrows, cairns, stones, hut clusters and tracks. The long earthworks on the moors to the north of Pickering may have been used for driving and rounding up animals.

Mysterious carved stones can be found, around Dod Law in Northumberland, for example, and on Ilkley Moor. There are also gigantic standing stones: the Devil's Arrows at Boroughbridge and the even taller Rudston monolith. The Brigantes were the Celtic people who occupied Northumberland, Yorkshire, Lancashire and Cumbria when the Romans came. At Stanwick are the fortifications where they made their last stand against Rome.

Museums of interest

Alnwick Castle Museum; Transport & Archaeology Museum, Hull; Manor House Museum, Ilkley; Dorman Museum, Middlesborough; University Museum of Antiquities, Newcastle upon Tyne; Scarborough Museum; City Museum, Sheffield; Whitby Literary & Philosophical Society Museum; Yorkshire Museum, York.

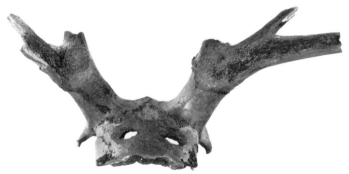

Headdress made of the skull and antlers of a red deer. Found at Star Carr, it was probably used in hunting or fertility magic and possibly also in stalking deer.

PLACES TO VISIT

Alkborough, Humberside

SE 881217. 'Julian's Bower' is a 40-ft (12-m) maze cut in the turf on a hillside to the W of the village, with an earthwork above. Games were played here on May Eve as late as the early nineteenth century. There is a copy of the maze in the floor of the church porch.

This tombstone in Alkborough churchyard has a miniature copy of the nearby maze called Julian's Bower, an interesting example of the Christian use of what was originally a pagan symbol.

Almondbury Castle Hill, West Yorkshire

SE 153141, on the outskirts of Huddersfield. The hillfort is partly obliterated by the ruins of the Norman castle. It was a stronghold of the Brigantes and possibly the place where their pro-Roman queen, Cartimandua, took refuge from her anti-Roman husband, King Venutius. The Victoria Tower, built here in 1897 in hour of a later queen, provides extensive views.

Alnham Castle Hill, Northumberland

NT 980109. Small Iron Age hillfort on the Cheviot slopes to the W of Alnham, defended by triple banks and ditches. At the NE are the remains of the huts and boundary walls of a later village.

Boltby Scar, North Yorkshire

SE 506857. Promontory fort of the late centuries BC on the sheer edge of the Hambleton Hills in the North York Moors National Park, SE of Boltby. The fort is on the Cleveland Way footpath, part of which follows the old drove road – along which cattle were driven down to London and the south – which earlier still was a prehistoric traders' track. Close by are mysterious 'dykes' or long earthworks, which may have been tribal boundaries or perhaps were used for driving and rounding up herds. There are many barrows along the Cleveland Way, among them **Kepwick Long Barrow** SE 493904, above Kepwick. It is 4 ft (1.2 m) high and 100 ft (30 m) long. In it were found 5 disarticulated skeletons, the bodies having been exposed to rot on a wooden platform before the bones were buried.

The Bull Stone, West Yorkshire

SE 206435, 1 mile (1.6 km) NE of Guiseley. This tapering standing stone, which was erected in about 2000 BC, is 6 ft (1.8 m) tall.

Danby Rigg, North Yorkshire

NZ 710065, 1 mile (1.6 km) S of Danby. Earthworks and a stone wall cut across this steep spur above Danby Dale in beautiful country in the North York Moors National Park. Between them there is a circular bank, 70 ft (21 m) in diameter. To the N of the stone wall are hundreds of small cairns, of uncertain significance – no burials have been found under them. A solitary stone is still standing, all that is left of a stone circle. There are traces of Celtic fields on the E slope. The various remains may date from periods between about 1700 BC and the first century AD.

Danes Dyke, Humberside

SE 216694. Despite the name, this impressive earthwork has nothing to do with the Danes. It is a bank, up to 18 ft (5.4 m) high, with a ditch 60 ft (18 m) wide, running for 2½ miles (4 km) and cutting off the peninsula of Flamborough Head, evidently for defence. It was probably built in the first century BC, and there is now a nature trail here.

Danes Graves, Humberside

TA 018633, 3 miles (4.8 km) N of Great Driffield, to E of B1249. The round barrows here are not the graves of Danes, but the remains of a large cemetery of the Parisi people, second century BC. One of the barrows, excavated in 1897, was found to contain the bodies of 2 men with a 2-wheeled chariot and horse harness, probably a chieftain accompanied by his charioteer, who was killed to go with his master to the land of the dead.

The three Devil's Arrows weigh more than 20 tons each and have been standing in a row in their man-sized sockets for about 4000 years. They may have been connected with fertility ritual.

Mysterious cup and ring marks and other patterns were pecked out on stones at Dod Law, probably in the Bronze Age.

The Devil's Arrows, North Yorkshire

SE 391666, at Boroughbridge, in fields close to the A1. These 3 huge stones (there were 4 of them in the seventeenth century) were dragged here with enormous effort from Knaresborough, over 6 miles (9.6 km) away, perhaps in about 2000 BC. Ranging from 18 ft to 22½ ft (5.5 to 6.8 m) in height, and weighing more than 20 tons each, they stand in a N/S line 570 ft (173 m) long. The deep grooves in the stones are thought to be the result of weathering. No one knows why they were placed here, but they may well have been linked with fertility ritual and were quite likely connected with the Thornborough complex of sacred sites to the N. Legend has it that these monstrous monoliths were arrows fired by the Devil, either at some old cities (shades of Sodom and Gomorrah) or at the early Christians in the nearby Brigantian town of Aldborough.

Dod Law, Northumberland

NU 004317. On this hill, SE of Doddington with a fine view over the River Till to the Cheviots, are the remains of a fortified settlement of the late centuries BC, with ramparts standing up to 9 ft (2.7 m) high, and the outlines of huts and cattle enclosures. Scattered about among all this are numerous carved rocks of much earlier date. About 1 mile (1.6 km) to the NE are the remains of more enclosures at **Ringses Camp** NU 013328.

Time has worn grooves and runnels in the blocks of local sandstone which were erected in a circle at Duddo in Northumberland.

Duddo, Northumberland

NT 931437. To the NW of the village, on a knoll, stands this impressive circle of 5 stones, up to 7½ ft (2.3 m) high. The circle is on private land and not accessible when crops are growing, but is visible from the cart track.

Duggleby Howe, North Yorkshire

SE 881669. Round barrow, SE of Duggleby, originally over 30 ft (9 m) high and still rising to 20 ft (6 m), and about 120 ft (36.5 m) across, containing altogether some 5000 tons of chalk, dating from about 2500 BC. Remains of more than 60 people were found when the barrow was excavated. Were many of them sacrificed at the funeral of a powerful chief, to serve him in the afterworld?

Eston Nab, Cleveland

NZ 568184, 3 miles (4.8 km) NW of Guisborough. There are fine views from this fort on the edge of a cliff in the Eston Hills, with ramparts up to 14 ft (4.2 m) high.

Folkton, North Yorkshire

TA 059777. The small barrow here, SE of Flixton, contained 3 strange objects which had been buried with a 5-year-old child, in about 1800 BC. They are small 'drums' made of chalk, carved with geometric patterns and stylized owlish eyes and eyebrows, possibly representing

A beautiful view of the Duddo circle on the skyline. There were probably more stones in the circle originally.

a mother goddess. Were they toys for a dearly loved child to play with in the afterworld, or protection against danger, or both? Nearby are more barrows, **Sharp Howes** TA 049777 rising to 8 ft (2.4 m).

Goatstones, Northumberland

NY 829748, off a track near the Ravenshaugh Crags, 3 miles (4.8 km) NW of Simonburn. A rectangle of 4 stones surrounds a family burial place. There are cup markings on the E stone. This type of monument is called a four-poster, and is more common in Scotland than in England.

Grassington, North Yorkshire

The moors which lie to the N of this attractive Wharfedale village are covered with prehistoric hut circles and field boundaries. **Lea Green** SE 004651, reached from Chapel Street, is the most interesting site.

The High Bridestones, North Yorkshire

NZ 850046, on Sleights Moor, SE of Grosmont. The stones here seem to be the remains of stone rows. Between them and the A169 road is **Flat Howe**, a round barrow with a kerb of stones. To the E of A169 on Bridestones Moor, the Low Bridestones (*National Trust*) are impressive outcrops of rock.

Holystone Common, Northumberland

NT 953020, S of Holystone. There are numerous cairns here, up to 60 ft (18 m) across, in which bodies were buried with flint tools, pins, urns and food vessels. To the W, on Harbottle Hill, is the 2000-ton mass of the **Drake Stone** or **Dragon Stone**, said to have been a sacred site in prehistoric times: sick children were passed over it to cure them until the nineteenth century. The **Lady's Well** at Holystone goes back to pre-Christian times and a 'lady' older than the Virgin Mary.

Ilkley, West Yorkshire

SE 115472. In the public gardens opposite St Margaret's church, protected by railings, are stones carved with hollows, circles and ladder patterns, brought from the moors to the S of the town, where there are about 40 carved rocks. A walk from the main street leads to Heber's Ghyll and on to the **Panorama Rocks** SE 104470 and the famous **Swastika Stone** SE 094470, on which is inscribed a double swastika twining round a group of hollows in the shape of a cross. This stone may be a thousand or more years later in date than the others, perhaps after 300 BC. Also richly carved are the **Hanging Stones** SE 124867. The **Twelve Apostles** SE 126451 form a circle 52 ft (15.8 m) in diameter, but many of the stones have fallen or been removed. The **Bradup** circle SE 090440, W of the road across the moor to Keighley, has 12 small stones.

Ingleborough Hill, North Yorkshire

SO 742746, can be reached by track from Ingleton, about 4

Stone inscribed with cup and ring marks at the hillfort of Lordenshaw. The most elaborate collections of patterns tend to occur on the most impressive stone slabs.

miles (6.4 km) away. Britain's highest hillfort, a stronghold of the Brigantes, with a single rampart built of stone blocks, crowns this desolate 2370-ft (790-m) summit in the Yorkshire Dales National Park. This area is well-known for its spectacular limestone caverns, with underground rivers, waterfalls, stalactites and stalagmites. Ingleborough Cavern, near Clapham, and the White Scar Caves, near Ingleton, have guided tours. Some of the 'green roads' across the moors were first trodden by prehistoric travellers. An example is **Mastiles Lane**, across Malham Moor, later a drove road and now a popular walking route. The **Druid's Altar** SO 949652, on Malham Moor, is the remains of a burial cairn.

Ingram, Northumberland

In a beautiful valley. Northumberland National Park information centre here. On the surrounding hills are barrows, hillforts and remains of villages of late pre-Roman and Roman times. The largest of these settlements is **Greaves Ash** NT 965164, near the 56-ft (18-m) waterfall called Linhope Spout.

Loose Howe, North Yorkshire

NZ 703008, on Danby High Moor, 5 miles (8 km) S of Danby. This barrow is 7 ft (2.1 m) high and 60 ft (18 m) across and concealed a remarkable burial of about 1700 BC. Inside the mound were 3 dugout canoes, each 9 ft (2.7 m) long. Two of them had been used as the coffin and its lid. The body had been dressed in a linen garment or shroud, with a pillow of grass or straw for the head. The remains of a leather shoe with lace holes were found, and a bronze dagger. The use of a boat as a coffin suggests a belief in a sea journey after death.

Lordenshaw, Northumberland

NZ 055993, off a minor road S of Rothbury, about 1 mile (1.6 km) from B6342. This small hillfort stands on

Cup and ring markings cluster on a large slab of rock at another Northumberland site, Roughting Linn.

moorland above the River Coquet, overlooking beautiful country. Inside are the outlines of circular huts, possibly dating from Roman times. On the path to the fort, and of much earlier date, are 2 rocks with cup and ring markings, and there are more carved rocks to the E of the fort, and cairns on the NE slope of the hill.

Close-up view of one of the maze-like figures at Roughting Linn. The meaning of these patterns is elusive, but they may be connected with belief in an afterlife.

Old Bewick, Northumberland

NU 075216. Iron Age hillfort on a steep spur to the E of Old Bewick, overlooking the River Breamish. The fort is curiously shaped, like a pair of spectacles. Nearby to the SE are rocks with cup and ring markings. Terrific views. To the N there are numerous cairns on **Hepburn Moor** NU 083231. At **Blawearie** NU 082223 is a ring of stones which were originally the wall of a burial mound.

Ross (or Ros) Castle, Northumberland

NU 081253, *National Trust*. This 1000-ft (304-m) hill has traces of a hillfort on the summit and magnificent views of the Cheviots, Bamburgh Castle and Lindisfarne. Just below is Chillingham Park, where a celebrated herd of wild white cattle can be viewed. These animals are the only ones of their kind never to have been crossed with domestic cattle and are descended directly from the prehistoric wild ox, *bos primigenius*.

Roughting (or Rowting) Linn, Northumberland

NT 984367, 2 miles (3.2 km) E of Ford. One of the most spectacular examples of prehistoric rock carving lies just to the W of the minor road from Lowick to Milfield over Bar Moor. The surface of a large sloping slab is covered

THE ENIGMA OF THE CARVED STONES

Maps of the sky? Charts of burial mounds or sacred sites? An early form of writing? Knife-sharpeners? Sundials? Doodles? Moulds for casting metal? Mortars for crushing grain? Equipment for a game of some kind? Stylized representations of a mother goddess? Cups and channels for catching and draining the blood of sacrifices?

All these explanations have been suggested to account for the mysterious cup marks and other patterns carved, or rather pecked out, on rocks in highland areas of Britain. The 'cups' are small hollows made in the stone (and need to be distinguished from natural marks and depressions). 'Cups and rings' are hollows surrounded by one or more circles. There are also spirals, branching lines, ladder patterns and meandering lines. It is possible that people had similar designs painted or tattooed on their bodies.

Most specimens of this abstract art are dated to approximately the period 2000 to 1000 BC, but the finest examples are older. They come from the great Stone Age tombs of Ireland, such as Newgrange, and the style may have spread from Ireland to Britain. In Northumberland and Yorkshire the designs are found on outcrops of rock on the moors. The most elaborate ones tend to be on the most impressive slabs of stone, commanding the largest views. The patterns are also found on stones in graves and there may be a link between the art and the dead, and perhaps with a belief in life after death. Do some of the patterns form a kind of map of the journey of the soul after death and towards rebirth?

The frequent appearances of the circle motif suggest a connection with the stream of ideas which produced the circular sacred sites, henges and stone circles of the Stone and Bronze Ages. It certainly seems likely that the baffling patterns have a symbolic, religio-magical meaning, though it eludes us. They retained a magical aura down into the nineteenth century. Milk was poured into the cups for the fairies, to keep their goodwill, and rainwater which collected in them was believed to have healing power and was used in the treatment of eye troubles and rheumatism, to banish warts and to relieve barrenness in women.

The monolith of millstone grit in Rudston churchyard is the tallest standing stone in England and stands as high as the nave of the church.

with more than 60 patterns, including cup marks, rings and maze-like figures. Immediately to the w are the ramparts and ditches of an Iron Age promontory fort. The linn, or waterfall, is outside the fort's NE corner.

Roulston Scar, North Yorkshire

SE 514816, on the Cleveland Way, 5 miles (8 km) E of Thirsk, s of A170. This large promontory fort covers some 53 acres (21 ha) and the rampart still stands up to 11 ft (3.3 m) high. There is a white horse on the hillside to the s, cut in 1857.

Rudston, Humberside

TA 097677. In the churchyard, towering up as high as the roof of the nave, is an enormous standing stone, the tallest in England, brought here in about 2000 BC from at least 10 miles (16 km) away to the N. It stands $25\frac{1}{2}$ ft (7.8 m) high and its weight is estimated at 26 tons. There is another stone, 3 ft (0.9 m) tall, in the NE of the churchyard and the remains of a stone cist. This was a sacred area in prehistoric times and air photography has revealed 3 cursuses here. The monolith may have been a landmark, to guide travellers to the area. The local story, however, is that the Devil hurled it at the church in a temper, but missed. About 3 miles (4.8 km) to the NW and of the same period is the giant, tree-shrouded barrow called **Willy Howe** TA 063724, 24 ft (7.2 m) high and 130 ft (40 m) across.

Stanhope, Durham

In the churchyard is the stump of a fossilized tree, which was alive 250,000 years ago. It was found in 1964 in a nearby quarry, and stands 7 ft (2.1 m) high. A path from the w of the town leads up Stanhope Dean to **Heathery Burn Cave**, where in the 1840s a wealth of equipment was found: spearheads, axes, a gold bracelet, a bronze bucket and horse harness (now in the British Museum).

Stanwick Camp, North Yorkshire

NZ 179112, *Dept of the Environment*, 3 miles (4.8 km) SW of Piercebridge, reached from Forcett. These extensive fortifications of the first century AD were excavated by Sir Mortimer Wheeler in the 1950s. The camp was the stronghold of King Venutius of the Brigantes, who tried to resist the Romans, while his queen, Cartimandua, was pro-Roman. Venutius finally led his people in revolt against Rome, but was crushed by the Ninth Legion, which marched north from York in AD 71. The centre and earliest part of the defences is the 17-acre (10-ha) fort known as the **Tofts**, to the s of Stanwick church, built early in the first century. In about AD 50 to 60 an area of around 130 acres (53 ha) to the N of the Tofts was protected by a new earthwork, and in about AD 70 another 600 acres (240 ha) to the s were walled off. The Roman infantry, however, were the most efficient fighting troops in the world in their time and these defences were not strong enough to hold them back. The Tofts itself was probably the site of the last stand of the Brigantes. A fine sword, nearly 3 ft (0.9 m) long in a scabbard of ash wood, was found here and also horse harness and chariot fittings.

The Three Kings, Northumberland

NT 774009, in the Redesdale Forest, near Byrness, reached by a track off the Forestry Drive. A 'four-poster', with 4 stones surrounding a cairn.

Part of the fortifications at Stanwick Camp, Britain's largest hillfort, where the Brigantes were crushed by the Roman Ninth Legion.

Horse trappings and chariot fittings found at Stanwick. The striking bronze representation of a horse's head is only a little over $3\frac{1}{4}$ in (9.5 cm) high.

Thornborough, North Yorkshire

SE 285795, 1 mile (1.6 km) NE of West Tanfield. The area to the N and E of Ripon, between the Ure and Swale rivers, was an important religious centre in about 2000 BC and 6 large henges were built here within 7 miles (11.2 km) of each other. The 3 at Thornborough are the least damaged by ploughing and the central one is the easiest to reach. They are in a straight line, orientated NW/SE, about $\frac{1}{2}$ mile (804 m) apart, each with entrances at the NW and SE. Each is surrounded by a bank, which originally had a ditch on both sides of it. The bank was coated with gypsum, to make it shine gleaming white like the henges of the south. Three more henges, spoiled by farming, lie to the E of Ripon, at **Hutton Moor** SE 353735, **Cana** SE 361718 and **Nunwick** SE 323747. Among the henges are many round barrows, the burial places of chiefs and their families, laid to rest in the sacred area.

Victoria Cave, North Yorkshire

SO 838650, almost 1500 ft (457 m) up in the side of Langcliffe Scar, 2 miles (3.2 km) NE of Settle on the road to Malham. The bones of prehistoric animals were found in the cave, including those of hippo, woolly rhino, elephant, bear and red deer. Groups of hunters sheltered here on occasion during the Old and Middle Stone Ages, leaving behind them flints, ivory tools and a harpoon made of deer antler. The cave was used again in Roman times, as was the **Jubilee Cave** nearby, which had been occupied in the New Stone Age. Some of the finds are in the Pig Yard Club Museum, Settle.

Yeavering Bell, Northumberland

NT 928294, 1 mile (1.6 km) SE of Kirknewton. The twin summits of this 1180-ft (359-m) hill on the edge of the Cheviots, commanding splendid views, are enclosed by the defences of a strong hillfort, a Brigantian township when the Romans came. The fort covers 13 acres (5 ha). Inside are the foundations of about 130 huts, anything from 18 to 30 ft (5.4 to 9 m) across. The main entrance to the fort is at the S. At the foot of the hill stood a royal palace of the seventh-century kings of Northumbria, but no trace of it is left. To the E are more hillforts: **Harehope Hill** NT 956285, 2 miles (3.2 km) W of Wooler, **Humbleton Hill** NT 966283, $1\frac{1}{2}$ miles (2.4 km) W of Wooler, and **The Kettle** NT 984273, a promontory fort 1 mile (1.6 km) S of Wooler.

The stone circle at Castlerigg, in a beautiful setting in the Lake District, may be one of the oldest in Britain.

THE NORTH-WEST
CUMBRIA, LANCASHIRE,
MERSEYSIDE, GREATER MANCHESTER

BEFORE the Romans came to England the Celtic inhabitants of the country did not call themselves Britons (the Roman name for them), but Cymry, meaning 'fellow countrymen', and the word survives in the name Cumbria. The area is best known for the mountain scenery of the Lake District, where glaciers aeons ago gouged out the deep valleys which are now made beautiful by lakes and waterfalls. Little evidence has survived of the early hunters in the north-west, but the farmers of the New Stone Age were settling here before 4000 BC, on the fertile soil along the coast, in the Furness peninsula and inland in the Eden valley, which became an important route for traders.

Far from being daunted by the Lake District mountains, the early settlers explored them and discovered types of rock from which sharp and durable edged tools could be made. Axe factories were set up, like the one at Pike of Stickle above Great Langdale, and higher still, almost on the summit of Scafell Pike, the highest peak in England.

The axes were brought down from the mountains and traded all over the country. The local farmers used them for clearing grazing for their cattle and pigs in the oak and elm forests on the hillsides. The process continued for centuries and the bare, rugged look of the Lake District today, so much admired as a piece of unspoiled natural landscape, is in reality the consequence of human action.

The most impressive prehistoric monuments in the north-west are the grey and weathered stone circles of Cumbria, which in their setting of moor and fell are among the most eerie and evocative in England. There are also hundreds of cairns and barrows on the lower fells and foothills, and the remains of villages, as on the moors near Crosby Ravensworth. Further south, much less has survived from the prehistoric age, but there are some attractive hillforts of the last centuries BC.

Museums of interest
Barrow in Furness Museum; Carlisle Museum & Art Gallery (Tullie House); Lancaster Museum; Merseyside County Museum, Liverpool; Manchester Museum; Harris Museum & Art Gallery, Preston.

Stone carvings of the heads of gods are among the most dramatic examples of Celtic art and demonstrate the Celtic fascination with the human head. The head with ram's horns (left), from Netherby, Cumbria, is now in the Carlisle Museum. The other, from Bradford in Yorkshire, is in the Manor House Museum, Ilkley.

The Castlerigg circle, with two massive stones flanking the entrance on the N side.

A complicated network of astronomical indications can be worked out from the circle.

PLACES TO VISIT

Birkrigg Common, Cumbria
SD 292739, 1 mile (1.6 km) W of Bardsea in the Furness peninsula. This double circle of small stones, known as the **Druids' Temple**, had an unusual feature, a cobbled floor. Pits containing cremated human remains were found inside the inner circle. On the common nearby are barrows and enclosures. At **Holme Bank** SD 276734, 1 mile (1.6 km) NW of Baycliff, are the remains of a fortified farmstead, probably occupied in the first century AD, with traces of huts. To the NW at Little Urswick is **Urswick Stone Walls** SD 260741, the remains of the huts and cattle pounds of settlements of the first century BC and the first century AD.

Bleasdale, Lancashire
SD 577460, in a wood to the NE of the church. The low mound of turf here was surrounded by a ring of 11 oak posts (now marked by concrete posts), with a ditch outside them, and outside this again a palisade of posts in a circle 150 ft (46 m) in diameter. In the mound was a grave, in which were 2 urns containing cremated human bones. The site, dating from about 1800 BC, may have been a shrine to two famous or powerful persons.

The Calderstones, Merseyside
SJ 407873, in Calderstones Park, Menlove Gardens, Liverpool. The stones are from a Neolithic grave which once stood at the mouth of the Mersey. They are marked with cups, rings, lozenges and spirals, and with footprints, which may have been added later.

Carrock Fell, Cumbria
NY 343337. This strong hillfort NW of Mungrisdale, possibly a stronghold of the Brigantes, demands a difficult, steep climb, best not attempted in bad weather. The fort is surrounded by a stone wall. Inside is a large cairn with a cist at the centre. There are many more cairns to the N.

Castercliffe Camp, Lancashire
SD 885384, 1 mile (1.6 km) E of Nelson. Behind triple ramparts is a hillfort with outworks at the E entrance.

Casterton, Cumbria
SD 640799, 1 mile (1.6 km) E of Casterton. Twenty small stones stand in a 59-ft (18-m) circle on a low platform. Date possibly about 2000 BC. There may have been a burial in the middle of the circle.

Castle Crag, Cumbria
NY 249159, *National Trust*, in Borrowdale in the Lake District. The fort on the crag, of late pre-Roman or Roman date, commands wonderful views of the Jaws of Borrowdale and across Derwentwater to Skiddaw. Nearby is the famous Bowder Stone, a huge rock weighing 2000 tons. Above the Watendlath stream, the fortified summit of **Reecastle Crag** NY 275175 (*National Trust*) also provides fine views. Another fort, **Castle Crag** NY 300188, rears up above Shoulthwaite Gill. These small forts commanded the pastures on the mountain slopes to which farmers drove their beasts in summer.

Castle How, Cumbria
NY 202308, E of Cockermouth, a small fort with strong defences on a rocky peninsula that projects into Bassenthwaite Lake.

Castlerigg Circle, The Carles or Keswick Carles, Cumbria
NY 292236, *Dept of the Environment* and *National Trust*, in a beautiful mountain landscape in the Lake District, off a minor road, 2 miles (3.2 km) E of Keswick. This may be one of the oldest stone circles in Britain. There are 38 stones in the circle, which is slightly flattened at the NE and is about 100 ft (30 m) across. It is also known as Druids' Circle. At the N entrance are 2 massive stones. Inside, on the E side are 10 stones arranged in an oblong, whose purpose is not understood. To the E is a hill called Threlkeld Knott, over which the sun rises at the spring and autumn equinoxes. To the SW is an outlying stone in the direction of the midwinter sunset, and a network of astronomical indications can be worked out from the circle. On the hillside to the E are cairns and the remains of a prehistoric settlement and field system, NY 329241. Fine views of Helvellyn, Skiddaw and other Lakeland peaks.

Chapeltown, Greater Manchester
SD 716159, 1 mile (1.6 km) W of Chapeltown. A circle of 6 or 7 stones, with an outlier to the SW. Further to the SW is another circle, of 2 concentric rings of stones. The stones in the centre probably mark a burial.

Crosby Garrett, Cumbria
NY 719064. To the W of Kirkby Stephen are the remains of 3 villages of the last centuries BC, with traces of huts and gardens or paddocks among fields, boundary banks and ancient tracks. Barrows to the E.

Crosby Ravensworth, Cumbria
The moors to the S are studded with pre-Roman village sites. At **Ewe Close** NY 609135 the stone huts had walls 6 ft (1.8 m) thick. At **Burwans** NY 621123 the walled

village has its gateway to the NW, from which the village street leads past the remains of circular huts, some with courtyards. There are traces of fields to the N and E. To the NW are the stone circles of **Castlehowe Scar** NW 587155 and **Oddendale** NY 593129.

Eskdale Moor, Cumbria
NY 173025. There are 5 stone circles on the moor, reached by a stiff climb from Boot, to the S. All of them enclose cairns containing cremations. The biggest circle is below the summit of Brats Hill. Its cairns contained burned human remains, animal bones and antlers.

Grey Croft, Cumbria
NY 034024, 1 mile (1.6 km) N of Seascale. The stone circle here was restored in 1949. It surrounds a cairn in which a cremated body was buried.

King Arthur's Round Table, Cumbria
NY 523284, *Dept of the Environment*, just S of Eamont

THE DRUIDS

Like many prehistoric monuments, the Castlerigg circle and the double circle on Birkrigg Common are popularly associated with the Druids. Whether there is any real connection is less certain and the picture of Druids as dignified white robed figures conducting stately rituals in stone circles is largely a modern fantasy. The real Druids were more like the shamans or medicine-men of tribal societies, and the Romans stamped them out in England and Wales because of their predilection for human sacrifice by stabbing, strangling and burning alive.

The Druids were the priests, wise men and lawgivers of the Celtic peoples in northern Europe. They had an awesome reputation, partly because of the human victims they sacrificed on altars drenched in blood and entrails, and partly because they were believed to have a profound understanding of astronomy, mathematics and science, beyond the reach of ordinary mortals.

The Druids did not build the great stone circles of England, which had been completed long before, but they do appear to have inherited something of the knowledge of the astronomer-priests of earlier times, including skill in the calendar and in herbs and medicines. Like their predecessors, probably, the Druids kept their knowledge secret and handed it down by word of mouth, enshrined in verses which had to be learned by heart. It was said to take 20 years to master the Druid secrets and commit them to memory. According to classical writers, the Druids performed their rites in forest clearings, enclosed by a palisade or a bank and ditch and containing rough wooden idols pallid with age. It may well be, however, that where they found the ancient stone circles conveniently to hand they would take advantage of them too.

Fanciful representation of an Archdruid from an early nineteenth-century book on costume which has exerted a powerful influence on romantic ideas about the Druids.

King Arthur's Round Table, near Penrith, is a circular henge with a ditch and bank marking off the sacred area. The site was much altered in the nineteenth century.

Bridge to E of A6, S of Penrith. Circular henge about 300 ft (91 m) across, with surrounding ditch and bank. To the W, on the other side of A6, is **Mayburgh** NY 519285 (*Dept of the Environment*), a larger sacred site, also circular, with a bank of boulders up to 15 ft (4.5 m) high. At the centre is a standing stone, the solitary survivor of 4, and 4 more once guarded the entrance at the E side. Both henges may date from about 2500 BC.

Long Meg and Her Daughters, Cumbria

NY 571373, 7 miles (11.2 km) NE of Penrith, off a minor road N of Little Salkeld, on sloping ground above the River Eden. This is one of the largest and finest stone circles in the country. There were originally about 70 stones, of which 27 are still standing, weighing on average 10 tons each. The largest weighs about 28 tons. Two

Near King Arthur's Round Table is another, larger henge, Mayburgh, which has a solitary standing stone at its centre.

bulky stones at the E and W sides may mark the spring and autumn equinoxes. Outside the circle to the SW is **Long Meg**, a standing stone 12 ft (3.6 m) tall, providing a sightline to the setting sun at the midwinter solstice. There are carvings on one side of Long Meg. Tradition has it that the stones were a witch and her coven, turned to stone by an early Christian saint, and it is said that they can never be counted more than once and give the same total. Wordsworth came here in 1821 and wrote a poem about the stones:

> A weight of awe, not easy to be borne,
> Fell suddenly upon my Spirit – cast
> From the dread bosom of the unknown past,
> When first I saw that family forlorn.

Nearby to the NE is **Little Meg** or the **Maughanby Circle** NY 577375 of 11 stones which originally surrounded a barrow: 2 of the stones have carvings on them.

Pike of Stickle, Cumbria

NY 272072, NW of Ambleside. On the steep, scree-strewn slopes of this mountain towering above Great Langdale in the Lake District are the remains of a busy axe factory, which was in operation from about 3000 to 1500 BC, probably working only in the summer. Its products found their way all over England, Scotland and Wales, carried principally by rivers and the sea. Many have been found in the south of England. Rough axeheads, flakes and chips can still be picked up here. High on the S side of the crag is a tiny cave, which may have been made by the Stone Age workmen.

Portfield Camp, Lancashire

SD 745355, 1 mile (1.6 km) SE of Whalley. Promontory fort with triple ramparts on the N, protected by steep hillsides on the SW and SE.

Long Meg and her Daughters form one of the finest stone circles in England.

Spiral pattern incised on one of the stones in the Little Meg circle, not far from Long Meg.

Shap, Cumbria

NY 567133, about 1 mile (1.6 km) S of Shap, on E side of A6, to N of the junction with B6261. There was a stone circle here, of which 6 fallen stones are left, more than 8 ft (2.4 m) long. The remains of an avenue of stones can be seen running away to the **Thunder Stone** NY 552157, to NW of Shap.

Swinside, Cumbria

SD 172883, 5 miles (8 km) W of Broughton in Furness, off track to Swinside Farm. An attractive circle of 55 smallish stones, 90 ft (27 m) in diameter. The stones are set close together and stand on a layer of pebbles, probably to stop them sinking into the earth. A distant memory of this probably inspired the story that attempts were made to build a church here, but the Devil made the stones sink below ground each night. This in turn gave the circle its name of Sunken Kirk.

Warton Crag, Lancashire

SD 492728, 1 mile (1.6 km) NW of Carnforth. Covered with trees, this hillfort is best visited in winter. It covers 15 acres (6 ha) on the S end of the hill, with steep drops on the SW and SE, and overlooks Morecambe Bay.

TABLE OF DATES

All the dates given here, down to the Roman invasion, are vague and tentative, and should be treated only as extremely rough indications. Fresh discoveries and new dating methods constantly alter the accepted chronology, pushing it further and further back.

12,000 BC	End of the Old Stone Age (Palaeolithic)
12,000–4500 BC	Middle Stone Age (Mesolithic)
8000 BC	The dog domesticated
7500 BC	Britain separated from the Continent
4500–2500 BC	New Stone Age (Neolithic)
4500 BC	Introduction of farming
4300 BC	Earliest causewayed camps and long barrows
3500 BC	Earliest henges
2800 BC	Stonehenge I – first phase
2750 BC	Early Beaker People arrive
2600 BC	Avebury and Silbury Hill
2500–1500 BC	Early Bronze Age
2100 BC	Stonehenge II – bluestone circles
2000 BC	Stonehenge IIIa – sarsen circle
1550 BC	Stonehenge in present form
1500–750 BC	Late Bronze Age
1000 BC	Earliest hillforts
750 BC	Iron Age begins
AD 43	Roman invasion of England

GLOSSARY OF ARCHAEOLOGICAL TERMS

Barrow (or **Tumulus**) a mound of earth over a burial, from an Old English word for a hill or hillock

Berm flat space between a barrow mound and its ditch or between the bank and ditch of a fort

Cairn a mound of stones heaped up over a burial, or a memorial or boundary marker

Capstone the stone which forms the roof of a burial chamber or cist

Causewayed camp Neolithic enclosure surrounded by one or more ditches interrupted by numerous 'causeways', with banks on the inside of the ditches

'Celtic' fields small rectangular fields, usually covering less than ½ acre (0.2 ha), dating from the Bronze Age to the end of the Roman period

Chambered tomb Neolithic tomb with one or more stone burial chambers covered over by a mound

Chert type of stone – a flint-like variety of quartz

Cist a stone coffin or a pit excavated in rock and used for a burial, usually covered over by a barrow or cairn

Cliff fort stronghold on a headland with earthworks across the landward approach

Cove a group of stones shaped like a U or a box, found inside some stone circles and henges: purpose in doubt, perhaps a shrine?

Cromlech the Welsh word for a dolmen

Cursus the Latin for 'racecourse': a long narrow avenue running between parallel banks and ditches; they were built in the New Stone Age, in association with long barrows, but their purpose is unknown

Dolmen a group of huge upright stones with a capstone on top, the remains of a Neolithic chambered tomb

Entrance grave type of Neolithic chambered tomb with a round mound found in Cornwall and the Isles of Scilly

Fogou underground passage, hiding place or store-cellar, found in Cornwall

Gallery grave Neolithic chambered tomb in which the entrance passage and the burial chamber are not clearly differentiated; there are some-times additional burial chambers off the gallery

Hand axe the all-purpose Stone Age implement for cutting, scraping and pounding; for use as an axe it was fastened to a haft

Henge Neolithic or Bronze Age circular enclosure surrounded by one or more banks and ditches, with the ditch usually being inside the bank, sometimes with a stone circle, setting of posts or wooden roundhouses inside (not all stone circles are henges, as not all have a surrounding bank and ditch)

Hillfort stronghold on a hill, defended by earthworks

Hut circle the stone foundations or lower courses of a prehistoric hut; the upper part may have been built of wood or stone

Long barrow trapezoidal or oblong mound over a Neolithic burial

Lynchet bank on a slope, formed by ploughed soil slipping downhill

Megalithic made of very large stones; the megalithic yard is a unit of measurement (2.72 ft/0.82 m) believed to have been used in the construction of stone circles

Mesolithic period the Middle Stone Age

Menhir old word for a single standing stone

Miz-maze a maze cut in turf

Neolithic period the New Stone Age

oppidum Latin for 'town', used for large Celtic lowland tribal centres, such as Colchester or St Albans

outlier a standing stone outside a stone circle and apparently related to it

Palaeolithic period the Old Stone Age

Passage grave chambered tomb with the burial chamber clearly distinguished from the entrance passage, covered by a round mound

Promontory fort hillfort on a steep spur with earthworks across its neck to bar the approach

Quoit Cornish word for a dolmen

Round barrow circular burial mound

Sarsen large sandstone boulder used in building burial chambers and stone circles

Tumulus old-fashioned term for a barrow, related to the Latin word for 'to swell'

ACKNOWLEDGMENTS

The publishers would like to thank the following for kindly supplying photographs and artwork for reproduction:

Aerofilms Ltd: endpapers, 25, 45, 46, 51, 52 right, 54 bottom, 55, 56, 59, 61, 71, 100, 118, 126

J & C Bord: frontispiece, 6, 18–19 bottom, 20 top, 20, 21, 27 bottom, 28, 31, 32, 34 top, 38 bottom, 39, 40 top, 48–9, 50 right, 53 bottom, 57 top, 58, 60 top, 62 top, 64, 66, 74–5, 78, 80, 84 top, 85 right, 86, 90, 93, 96 top, 96 bottom, 98–9, 101 top, 102, 104, 106, 111 bottom, 114 top, 116 top, 116 bottom, 117, 119, 121, 122–3, 124, 125, 131, 133, 136 top, 136 bottom, 144 bottom, 145 top, 145 bottom

British Museum: 11 bottom, 12 bottom left, 91 right, 95 left, 108 bottom right, 129

Jeffrey Burn: 8, 24, 30, 70, 77, 87, 95, 109

Cambridge University Collection: 22, 53 top, 57 bottom, 63 bottom, 84, 94, 111 top

Cambridge University Museum of Archaeology: copyright page

Carlisle Museum: 139 left

City of Bristol Museum and Art Gallery: 9 bottom left

Peter Clayton: 54 top, 91 left

Department of the Environment: 33 bottom, 108 top left

Elsevier/Phaidon: 65 left

Robert Estall: 26, 34 bottom, 35 top, 36–7, 42, 44 right, 47 right, 52 bottom, 60 bottom, 62 bottom, 69 left, 73, 82, 88, 110, 128, 131 top, 140–1

ET Archives: 8 middle, 8 bottom, 10 right, 13, 33 middle, 43 left, 43 right

Michael Holford: 9 top, 11 right, 105 left, 113

Her Majesty's Stationery Office: 50 left

Ronald Jessup: 69 right

Manor House Museum, Ilkley: 139 right

S & O Mathews: 29 top, 38 top, 44 bottom, 68, 69 right, 83, 126

Museum of London: 15 top

National Trust: 72

Cressida Pemberton-Pigott: 144 top

Pictorial Colour Slides: 10 left, 108 top left

Alan Saville: 79

Ronald Sheridan: 12 bottom right, 14, 29 bottom, 67 right, 67 left, 105 right, 134, 135

Mick Sharp: 17, 23 top, 33 top, 35 bottom, 40 bottom, 41, 63 top, 81 top, 85 left, 88, 89, 101 bottom, 132 bottom

Edwin Smith: 23 bottom, 27 top, 114 bottom, 115, 120, 131 bottom, 132 top, 138

Somerset Levels Project: 76 left, 76 right

Thames & Hudson: 30

Truro Museum (Royal Institute of Cornwall): 12 top

Vatican Museum (Alinari): 107

Weidenfeld & Nicolson: 65 bottom, 143

Derek Widdicombe: 112

INDEX